MORE
BANANA-
GRAMS!®

AN OFFICIAL BOOK

BY JOE EDLEY

AND
THE CREATORS
OF

WORKMAN PUBLISHING • NEW YORK

Copyright © 2010 Bananagrams

Puzzles by Joe Edley

Library of Congress Cataloging-in-Publication Data is available

ISBN 978-0-7611-5843-1

Workman books are available at special discounts when purchased in bulk for premiums and sales promotions as well as for fund-raising or educational use. Special editions or book excerpts also can be created to specification. For details, contact the Special Sales Director at the address below or send an e-mail to specialsales@workman.com.

Design by Rae Ann Spitzenberger

Bananagrams® is a trademark owned by Abe Nathanson doing business as Bananagrams, registered U.S. Patent and Trademark Office.

Photo © Olga Shelego

WORKMAN PUBLISHING COMPANY, INC.
225 Varick Street
New York, NY 10014-4381
www.workman.com

Printed in the United States of America
First printing March 2010

10 9 8 7 6 5 4 3 2 1

WELCOME TO BANANAGRAMS

THE STORY OF BANANAGRAMS

People everywhere have fallen for **Bananagrams,** the addictive craze that started as a simple idea: "An **anagram** game that is so fast it will drive you **bananas**!" And why not? It's amazingly fun and easy to play—you pick lettered tiles and create a grid of connecting and intersecting words as fast as you can.

It all began one summer when three generations of our family were vacationing together on the beach. We wanted a game that everybody—no matter their age—could enjoy. After marathon sessions playing and experimenting with various permutations of word games, we ended up inventing Bananagrams. Our family was hooked—and so we decided to share our new creation with everyone. The next thing we knew the game was named Game of the Year. Not bad for a rainy day invention.

We've took it to the next level with *Bananagrams! The Official Book*, and now we're very excited to present *More Bananagrams!* This book is loaded with hundreds of new puzzles that promise hours of brain-twisting word play. We've worked again with Joe Edley, who is both a master Bananagrammer and the only three-time National Scrabble Champion in history. He's employed his unparalleled anagramming skills to carefully craft these smart puzzles, and this book offers tons of new and exciting challenges that will thrill solvers of all stripes. So even if you've never grabbed a tile from a Bananagrams pouch, you're sure to find these puzzles very a-*peel*-ing!

HOW TO PLAY

Like the game, the puzzles in *More Bananagrams!* are fast and fun. In all, there are 8 puzzle categories—some offer one big challenge, while others feature a group of shorter problems to solve. Each puzzle is ranked by difficulty, ranging from one banana (easy) to five bananas (extra extra hard).

The farther you go into the book the harder the puzzles get, so dive in wherever you feel comfortable. If you're a beginner, you might want to try solving the puzzles with a pencil, since you may need to cross off tiles more than once. But if you're feeling brave, grab a pen!

All of the puzzles can be solved using common English words that appear in any standard dictionary. We've included a list of **Weords** (weird words!) on the facing page which we've compiled especially for Bananagrams players. This list features fun and unusual words that can come in very handy when you get stuck solving a puzzle. Oh, and just for fun, on page 10, you'll find a list of popular rule variations for those who are looking for new and clever ways to play Bananagrams, the game. Flip to the back of the book for the answer key which starts on page 270. You'll notice that some of the puzzles have multiple solutions; in these cases the key gives only one of the many possible answers. If you find a different one, good for you—you've earned some bragging rights!

We hope you'll dive right in and start solving. Have fun and don't be surprised if these puzzles drive you bananas!

Abe, Rena, Ava and Aaron Nathanson
The creators of Bananagrams

WEORDS!

These **WEORDS** (weird words!) are strange and useful
words that can help you be a better Bananagrammer. Have
a bunch full of A s and O s and U s? Or maybe you need the
perfect 3-letter word that starts with Y to finish your grid?
These lists of handy and unusual words can help get you out
of many a Bananagrams jam!

2-LETTER WORDS

AA	AY	ES	IT	NE	OY	UP
AB	BA	ET	JO	NO	PA	US
AD	BE	EX	KA	NU	PE	UT
AE	BI	FA	KI	OD	PI	WE
AG	BO	FE	LA	OE	QI	WO
AH	BY	GO	LI	OF	RE	XI
AI	DE	HA	LO	OH	SH	XU
AL	DO	HE	MA	OI	SI	YA
AM	ED	HI	ME	OM	SO	YE
AN	EF	HM	MI	ON	TA	YO
AR	EH	HO	MM	OP	TI	ZA
AS	EL	ID	MO	OR	TO	
AT	EM	IF	MU	OS	UH	
AW	EN	IN	MY	OW	UM	
AX	ER	IS	NA	OX	UN	

3-LETTER WORDS

AAH	ACT	AGA	AID	ALA	AMA	ANI
AAL	ADD	AGE	AIL	ALB	AMI	ANT
AAS	ADO	AGO	AIM	ALE	AMP	ANY
ABA	ADS	AGS	AIN	ALL	AMU	APE
ABS	ADZ	AHA	AIR	ALP	ANA	APO
ABY	AFF	AHI	AIS	ALS	AND	APP
ACE	AFT	AHS	AIT	ALT	ANE	APT

ARB	BED	BUY	CUP	DOM	EMS	FIB
ARC	BEE	BYE	CUR	DON	EMU	FID
ARE	BEG	BYS	CUT	DOR	END	FIE
ARF	BEL	CAB	CWM	DOS	ENG	FIG
ARK	BEN	CAD	DAB	DOT	ENS	FIL
ARM	BES	CAM	DAD	DOW	EON	FIN
ARS	BET	CAN	DAG	DRY	ERA	FIR
ART	BEY	CAP	DAH	DUB	ERE	FIT
ASH	BIB	CAR	DAK	DUD	ERG	FIX
ASK	BID	CAT	DAL	DUE	ERN	FIZ
ASP	BIG	CAW	DAM	DUG	ERR	FLU
ASS	BIN	CAY	DAN	DUH	ERS	FLY
ATE	BIO	CEE	DAP	DUN	ESS	FOB
ATT	BIS	CEL	DAW	DUO	ETA	FOE
AUK	BIT	CEP	DAY	DUP	ETH	FOG
AVA	BIZ	CHI	DEB	DYE	EVE	FOH
AVE	BOA	CIG	DEE	EAR	EWE	FON
AVO	BOB	CIS	DEF	EAT	EYE	FOP
AWA	BOD	COB	DEL	EAU	FAB	FOR
AWE	BOG	COD	DEN	EBB	FAD	FOU
AWL	BOO	COG	DEV	ECU	FAN	FOX
AWN	BOP	COL	DEW	EDH	FAR	FOY
AXE	BOS	CON	DEX	EDS	FAS	FRO
AYE	BOT	COO	DEY	EEK	FAT	FRY
AYS	BOW	COP	DIB	EEL	FAX	FUB
AZO	BOX	COR	DID	EFF	FAY	FUD
BAA	BOY	COS	DIE	EFS	FED	FUG
BAD	BRA	COT	DIF	EFT	FEE	FUN
BAG	BRO	COW	DIG	EGG	FEH	FUR
BAH	BRR	COX	DIM	EGO	FEM	GAB
BAL	BUB	COY	DIN	EKE	FEN	GAD
BAM	BUD	COZ	DIP	ELD	FER	GAE
BAN	BUG	CRU	DIS	ELF	FES	GAG
BAP	BUM	CRY	DIT	ELK	FET	GAL
BAR	BUN	CUB	DOC	ELL	FEU	GAM
BAS	BUR	CUD	DOE	ELM	FEW	GAN
BAT	BUS	CUE	DOG	ELS	FEY	GAP
BAY	BUT	CUM	DOL	EME	FEZ	GAR

HOT	JEE	KOA
HOW	JET	KOB
HOY	JEU	KOI
HUB	JEW	KOP
HUE	JIB	KOR
HUG	JIG	KOS
HUH	JIN	KUE
HUM	JOB	KYE
HUN	JOE	LAB
HUP	JOG	LAC
HUT	JOT	LAD
HYP	JOW	LAG
ICE	JOY	LAM
ICH	JUG	LAP
ICK	JUN	LAR
ICY	JUS	LAS
IDS	JUT	LAT
IFF	KAB	LAV
IFS	KAE	LAW
IGG	KAF	LAX
ILK	KAS	LAY
ILL	KAT	LEA
IMP	KAY	LED
INK	KEA	LEE
INN	KEF	LEG
INS	KEG	LEI
ION	KEN	LEK
IRE	KEP	LES
IRK	KEX	LET
ISM	KEY	LEU
ITS	KHI	LEV
IVY	KID	LEX
JAB	KIF	LEY
JAG	KIN	LIB
JAM	KIP	LID
JAR	KIR	LIE
JAW	KIS	LIN
JAY	KIT	LIP

GAS	GNU	HAE	HEW
GAT	GOA	HAG	HEX
GAY	GOB	HAH	HEY
GED	GOD	HAJ	HIC
GEE	GOO	HAM	HID
GEL	GOR	HAO	HIE
GEM	GOS	HAP	HIM
GEN	GOT	HAS	HIN
GET	GOX	HAT	HIP
GEY	GUL	HAW	HIS
GHI	GUM	HAY	HIT
GIB	GUN	HEH	HMM
GID	GUT	HEM	HOB
GIE	GUV	HEN	HOD
GIG	GUY	HEP	HOE
GIN	GYM	HER	HOG
GIP	GYP	HES	HON
GIT	HAD	HET	HOP

LIS	MIL	NET	OHM	OPS	OXO	PEA
LIT	MIM	NEW	OHO	OPT	OXY	PEC
LOB	MIR	NIB	OHS	ORA	PAC	PED
LOG	MIS	NIL	OIL	ORB	PAD	PEE
LOO	MIX	NIM	OKA	ORC	PAH	PEG
LOP	MOA	NIP	OKE	ORE	PAL	PEH
LOT	MOB	NIT	OLD	ORS	PAM	PEN
LOW	MOC	NIX	OLE	OSE	PAN	PEP
LOX	MOD	NOB	OMS	OUD	PAP	PER
LUG	MOG	NOD	ONE	OUR	PAR	PES
LUM	MOL	NOG	ONO	OUT	PAS	PET
LUV	MOM	NOH	ONS	OVA	PAT	PEW
LUX	MON	NOM	OOH	OWE	PAW	PHI
LYE	MOO	NOO	OOT	OWL	PAX	PHT
MAC	MOP	NOR	OPE	OWN	PAY	PIA
MAD	MOR	NOS				
MAE	MOS	NOT				
MAG	MOT	NOW				
MAN	MOW	NTH				
MAP	MUD	NUB				
MAR	MUG	NUN				
MAS	MUM	NUS				
MAT	MUN	NUT				
MAW	MUS	OAF				
MAX	MUT	OAK				
MAY	MYC	OAR				
MED	NAB	OAT				
MEG	NAE	OBA				
MEL	NAG	OBE				
MEM	NAH	OBI				
MEN	NAM	OCA				
MET	NAN	ODA				
MEW	NAP	ODD				
MHO	NAW	ODE				
MIB	NAY	ODS				
MIC	NEB	OES				
MID	NEE	OFF				
MIG	NEG	OFT				

Did You Know?

• Banana peels can be used to get rid of warts.

• Rubbing a banana peel on a mosquito bite helps reduce itching.

• In the Pacific Islands, banana leaves are used to treat burns.

• Bananas have a natural antacid effect on the body. Eating a banana can help alleviate heartburn.

• Research shows that just two bananas provide a body with enough energy for a strenuous 90-minute workout.

PIC	RAD	ROE	SHY	TAB	TON	VAR
PIE	RAG	ROM	SIB	TAD	TOO	VAS
PIG	RAH	ROT	SIC	TAE	TOP	VAT
PIN	RAI	ROW	SIM	TAG	TOR	VAU
PIP	RAJ	RUB	SIN	TAJ	TOT	VAV
PIS	RAM	RUE	SIP	TAM	TOW	VAW
PIT	RAN	RUG	SIR	TAN	TOY	VEE
PIU	RAP	RUM	SIS	TAO	TRY	VEG
PIX	RAS	RUN	SIT	TAP	TSK	VET
PLY	RAT	RUT	SIX	TAR	TUB	VEX
POD	RAW	RYA	SKA	TAS	TUG	VIA
POH	RAX	RYE	SKI	TAT	TUI	VID
POI	RAY	SAB	SKY	TAU	TUN	VIE
POL	REB	SAC	SLY	TAV	TUP	VIG
POO	REC	SAD	SOB	TAW	TUT	VIM
POP	RED	SAE	SOD	TAX	TUX	VIS
POT	REE	SAG	SOL	TEA	TWA	VOE
POW	REF	SAL	SOM	TED	TWO	VOW
POX	REG	SAP	SON	TEE	TYE	VOX
PRO	REI	SAT	SOP	TEG	UDO	VUG
PRY	REM	SAU	SOS	TEL	UGH	VUM
PSI	REP	SAW	SOT	TEN	UKE	WAB
PST	RES	SAX	SOU	TET	ULU	WAD
PUB	RET	SAY	SOW	TEW	UMM	WAE
PUD	REV	SEA	SOX	THE	UMP	WAG
PUG	REX	SEC	SOY	THO	UNS	WAN
PUL	RHO	SEE	SPA	THY	UPO	WAP
PUN	RIA	SEG	SPY	TIC	UPS	WAR
PUP	RIB	SEI	SRI	TIE	URB	WAS
PUR	RID	SEL	STY	TIL	URD	WAT
PUS	RIF	SEN	SUB	TIN	URN	WAW
PUT	RIG	SER	SUE	TIP	URP	WAX
PYA	RIM	SET	SUK	TIS	USE	WAY
PYE	RIN	SEW	SUM	TIT	UTA	WEB
PYX	RIP	SEX	SUN	TOD	UTE	WED
QAT	ROB	SHA	SUP	TOE	UTS	WEE
QIS	ROC	SHE	SUQ	TOG	VAC	WEN
QUA	ROD	SHH	SYN	TOM	VAN	WET

WHA	WOK	WYN	YAY	YIP	YUM	ZEP
WHO	WON	XIS	YEA	YOB	YUP	ZIG
WHY	WOO	YAG	YEH	YOD	ZAG	ZIN
WIG	WOS	YAH	YEN	YOK	ZAP	ZIP
WIN	WOT	YAK	YEP	YOM	ZAS	ZIT
WIS	WOW	YAM	YES	YON	ZAX	ZOA
WIT	WRY	YAP	YET	YOU	ZED	ZOO
WIZ	WUD	YAR	YEW	YOW	ZEE	ZUZ
WOE	WYE	YAW	YIN	YUK	ZEK	ZZZ

WORDS WITH A LOT OF VOWELS

AA	AUDIO	LOUIE	OIDIA	ROUE
AALII	AURA	LUAU	OLEA	TOEA
ADIEU	AURAE	MEOU	OLEO	UNAI
AE	AUREI	MIAOU	OLIO	UNAU
AECIA	AUTO	MOUE	OORIE	URAEI
AEON	AWEE	OBIA	OOZE	UREA
AERIE	BEAU	OBOE	OURIE	UVEA
AERO	CIAO	OE	OUZO	ZOEA
AGEE	EASE	OGEE	QUAI	ZOEAE
AGIO	EAU	OI	QUEUE	
AGUE	EAUX			
AI	EAVE			
AIDE	EERIE			
AIOLI	EIDE			
AJEE	EMEU			
AKEE	EPEE			
ALAE	ETUI			
ALEE	EURO			
ALOE	IDEA			
AMIA	ILEA			
AMIE	ILIA			
ANOA	INIA			
AQUA	IOTA			
AREA	IXIA			
ARIA	JIAO			
ASEA	LIEU			

Did You Know?

• Scientists believe bananas have grown on this planet for more than one million years.

• During the 17th and 18th centuries, it was considered bad luck to carry bananas on board sailing ships.

• As many as two million tons of bananas are imported into the United States each year.

WORDS WITH NO VOWELS

BRR	HMM	RHYTHM(S)	SYPH(S)
BY(S)	HYMN(S)	RYND(S)	SYZYGY
CRWTH	HYP(S)	SCRY	THY
CRY	LYMPH(S)	SH	THYMY
CRYPT(S)	LYNCH	SHY	TRY
CWM	LYNX	SHYLY	TRYST(S)
CYST(S)	MM	SKY	TSK
DRY(S)	MY	SLY	TYPP(S)
DRYLY	MYC(S)	SLYLY	TYPY
FLY	MYRRH(S)	SPRY	WHY(S)
FLYBY(S)	MYTH(S)	SPRYLY	WRY
FLYSCH	MYTHY	SPY	WRYLY
FRY	NTH	STY	WYCH
GHYLL(S)	NYMPH(S)	STYMY	WYN(S)
GLYCYL(S)	PLY	SYLPH(S)	WYND(S)
GLYPH(S)	PRY	SYLPHY	WYNN(S)
GYM(S)	PST	SYN	XYLYL(S)
GYP(S)	PSYCH(S)	SYNC(S)	XYST(S)
GYPSY	PYGMY	SYNCH(S)	ZZZ
HM	PYX	SYNTH(S)	

Q WORDS WITH NO U

FAQIR(S)	QANAT(S)	QIS
MBAQANGA(S)	QAT(S)	QOPH(S)
QABALA(S)	QI	QWERTY(S)
QABALAH(S)	QINDAR(S)	SHEQALIM
QADI(S)	QINDARKA	SHEQEL(S)
QAID(S)	QINTAR(S)	TRANQ(S)

OTHER WAYS TO PLAY

For all of you who've mastered the basic Bananagrams game and are itching for new ways to play, we're including some popular variations of the game that will help hone your Bananagramming skills.

BANANA SMOOTHIE

To play this less hectic version of the game, place all of the tiles face down and divided them equally among the players. Play the game as you normally would, except instead of peeling or dumping, each player uses only the tiles they've been given. The first player to use up all of their letters says "Bananas!" and is the winner. If the game ends in a stalemate, the player with the fewest remaining tiles wins.

BANANA SOLITAIRE

To play the game by yourself, place all of the tiles face down on the table. Take 21 tiles and play the game as you normally would. Only peel when you've used up your existing tiles. See how long it takes you to use up all 144 tiles, and then try to beat your own best time. Or challenge yourself by trying to make as few words as you can with all 144 letters.

BANANA NUMBERS

In this version, all of the rules of the regular game apply. However, instead of using any words they can, players must use a certain number of words or words that are of a certain length. For instance, you could say that each player can only have four words in their grid or only use words that are 4 letters long. The longer the words or the fewer words allowed in a grid, the harder the game.

BANANA THEMES

Play the game as you normally would, but instead of using any words they can, players must include in their grid at least one word related to a given theme. To make this even more challenging, require players to use two or three (or more!) themed words. Here are some fun ideas for themes: Names of family members, friends, famous people; objects in the room holiday words; animals; sports; clothing; winter, spring, summer, or fall words; buildings; parts of the body; school; politics; nature; words related to a specific movie, TV show, or book.

BEST BANANA

Divide the tiles evenly among all players. Then, instead of making word grids, have each player try to spell the longest word they can using the tiles they have. Instead of finding the longest word, you can make this a contest to spell the most words, the most unusual words, or even the all-around best words (though judging these can often turn into quite a battle!).

BANANAS ON BOARD

Play the game as you normally would, except limit the sprawl of the word grids. For instance, you could say that each player's grid must fit into a 10×10 tile space or you could rip out sheets of notepaper and use them as "boards." This forces a more condensed playing area and makes the game more challenging.

BANANA CLUES

Play the game as you normally would. At the end, have each player write out a clue for every word that appears in their finished grid. Then everyone passes their clue sheet and their bunch of mixed-up tiles to the player on their right. Using the tiles and clue sheet that were passed to them, each player must try to re-create the grid that the original player formed.

MORE BANANA-GRAMS!®

THE PUZZLES

For each bunch below, rearrange the letters to form two intersecting words that fit into the corresponding grid.

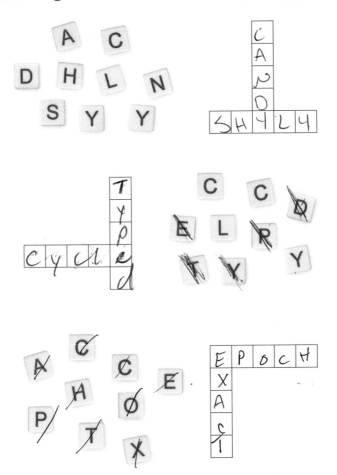

For each of the six words below, add one letter from the word HELIUM (each letter will be used only once) and then rearrange the letters to spell a kind of mammal. Once you've filled in all the blanks, take the shaded letters from each line and rearrange them to spell a bonus mammal.

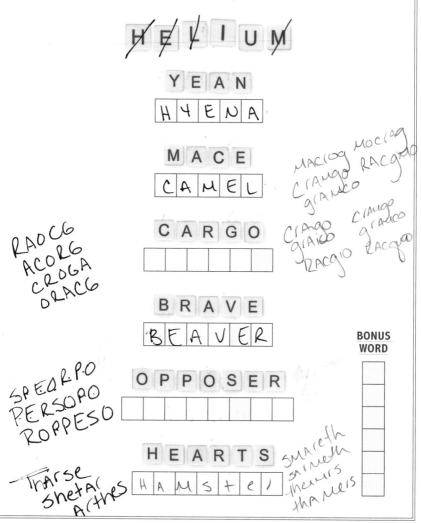

H~~E~~ ~~L~~ I U M

Y E A N
H Y E N A

M A C E
C A M E L

MACIOg MOCIAg
CIAugo RACgIO
gRAuco

C A R G O
[ ][ ][ ][ ][ ]

RAOCg
ACOR6
CROGA
ORAC6

CIAugo CIAugo
graico graico
RACgio RACgio

B R A V E
B E A V E R

BONUS WORD
[ ]
[ ]
[ ]
[ ]
[ ]
[ ]

SPEARPO
PERSORO
ROPPESO

O P P O S E R
[ ][ ][ ][ ][ ][ ][ ]

H E A R T S
H A M S T E R

Tharse
Shetar
Acthes

sMAreth
srineth
theurs
thaneis

15

For each of the three words below, change one letter to an A and then rearrange the letters to spell a type of dance.

A B Y̶ SM
（A above Y）

S A M B A

A̶ ̶T̶ N G O T
（A before, T crossed out）

T A N G O

B̶A̶ C̶ L A S S

S A L S A

For each of the three words below, change one letter to an N and then rearrange the letters to spell a part of the body.

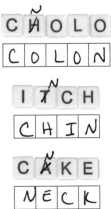

C H̶ O L O
（N above H）

C O L O N

I T̶ C H
（N above T）

C H I N

C A̶ K E
（N above A）

N E C K

Replace each of the question marks below with one of the five letters V, W, Y, F or ~~H~~ and then rearrange the letters to form a common word. Each of the five letters will be used only once.

A F K L ?

| | | | | |

C E K R ?

| | | | | |

A E N V ?

| H | A | V | E | N |

A D I O ?

| | | | | |

B E I T ?

| | | | | |

17

BANANA TREES

LEVEL

Use the 15 tiles in this bunch to create words that fit into the grids below. You will reuse this bunch for each of the four grids. The BANANA BITES provide hints to help you solve each grid.

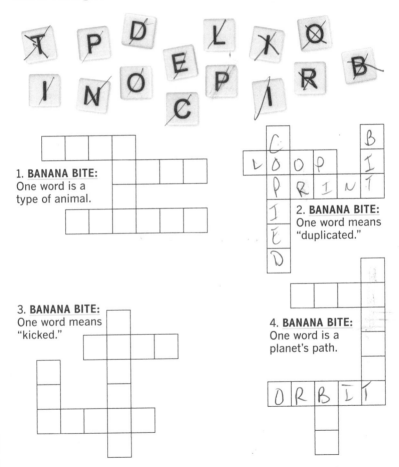

1. BANANA BITE:
One word is a type of animal.

2. BANANA BITE:
One word means "duplicated."

3. BANANA BITE:
One word means "kicked."

4. BANANA BITE:
One word is a planet's path.

18

Use the 15 tiles in this bunch to create words that fit into the grids below. You will reuse this bunch for each of the four grids. The BANANA BITES provide hints to help you solve each grid.

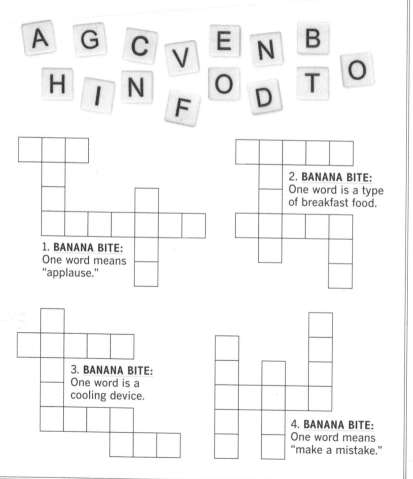

2. BANANA BITE:
One word is a type of breakfast food.

1. BANANA BITE:
One word means "applause."

3. BANANA BITE:
One word is a cooling device.

4. BANANA BITE:
One word means "make a mistake."

LEVEL

There is <u>one letter</u> that when added to all of the four-letter words below can be used to form new five-letter words. Find the letter that works for all four words, add it to each word, and then rearrange each set of letters to form a new word. For example, L can be added to ROADS, WEARY, EPICS and GONER to form DORSAL, LAWYER, SPLICE and LONGER.

COMMON
LETTER

T O O T

T H O U

T H E Y

R O O T

For each of the words below, replace one letter with the tile after the plus sign. Then rearrange the letters to spell a type of fruit.

MAUL + P

GIN + F

ARCHER + Y

CORNEA + G

ISLE + M

WICK + I

PACED + H

Add a B to each of the words below and then rearrange the letters in each word to form a new six-letter word.

A B I D E

[ ][ ][ ][ ][ ][ ]

C A N O E

[ ][ ][ ][ ][ ][ ]

H A L E R

[ ][ ][ ][ ][ ][ ]

C E D A R

[ ][ ][ ][ ][ ][ ]

Using any letters EXCEPT the ones that appear in the bunch below, fill in the blanks to form three new words.

E O I M R B

[ ][ ] L A T E

[ ][ ] V I C E

[ ][ ] T I L E

Using three of the tiles from each bunch on the left, fill in the blanks on the right to make a six-letter word that connects the grid.

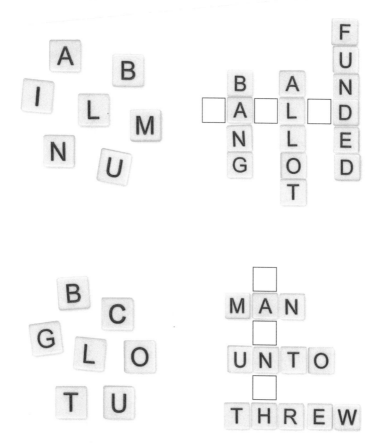

BUNCH OF BANANAS

LEVEL

For each word or phrase below, rearrange the letters to spell two new words that are both kinds of creatures. For example, FLOORING becomes FROG and LION.

E A R L O B E

[ ] [ ] [ ] [ ]   [ ] [ ] [ ] [ ] [ ]

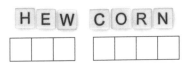

H E W   C O R N

[ ] [ ] [ ] [ ]   [ ] [ ] [ ] [ ] [ ]

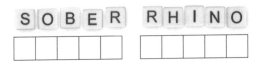

S O B E R   R H I N O

[ ] [ ] [ ] [ ] [ ]   [ ] [ ] [ ] [ ] [ ]

F A R E B O X

[ ] [ ] [ ] [ ]   [ ] [ ] [ ] [ ] [ ]

D E R O G A T E

[ ] [ ] [ ] [ ] [ ]   [ ] [ ] [ ] [ ]

Each set of 15 tiles below contains three common five-letter words. The letters of the first five-letter word are adjacent, but not in order. Find them and rearrange them to spell a word. Cross out those letters and imagine that the 10 remaining letters are now consecutive. Find five more adjacent letters that can be rearranged into the second word and then cross them out. The remaining five letters can now be rearranged to spell the final word.

Example: GANKNRNOTFHITIC. FRONT is the first word, which leaves GANKNHITIC. THINK is the second word, which leaves GANIC. That can be unscrambled into ACING.

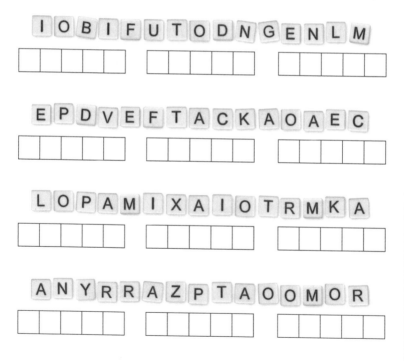

LEVEL

Use all 21 tiles in this bunch to create a collection of connecting and intersecting common words in the grid below. **Any word that has more than two letters must spell a number.** The words may be horizontal or vertical, reading left to right or top to bottom.

Use all 21 tiles in this bunch to create a collection of connecting and intersecting common words in the grid below. **Any word that has more than two letters must be the name of a planet.** The words may be horizontal or vertical, reading left to right or top to bottom.

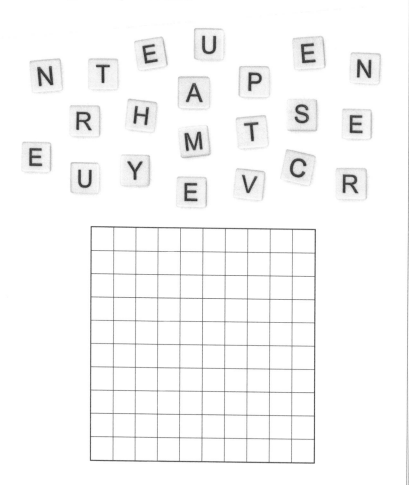

BANANA BOATS

LEVEL

For each of the word groups below, change one letter in the top word to one of the letters that appears in the bottom word, then rearrange the tiles to form a new common word. Do the same with each new word until you arrive at the bottom word. For example, a path from BARK to PLUM is BARK, MARK, RAMP, RUMP, PLUM.

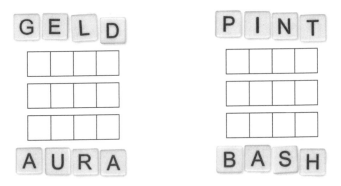

Each of the two-letter words below may be extended both on the right and the left to form a six-letter word. Drawing from the tiles directly above each word, fill in the blanks to find the longer words as quickly as you can.

C E G L N O Y
☐ ☐ A T ☐ ☐

D E H M O P R
☐ ☐ I T ☐ ☐

A B E I T U U
☐ ☐ R E ☐ ☐

C L M O T U U
☐ ☐ T O ☐ ☐

E I L O P R V
☐ ☐ A B ☐ ☐

For each bunch below, rearrange the letters to form two intersecting words that fit into the corresponding grid.

For each of the six words below, add one letter from the word **PUNIER** (each letter will be used only once) and then rearrange the letters to spell a breed of dog. Once you've filled in all the blanks, take the shaded letters from each line and rearrange them to spell a bonus breed.

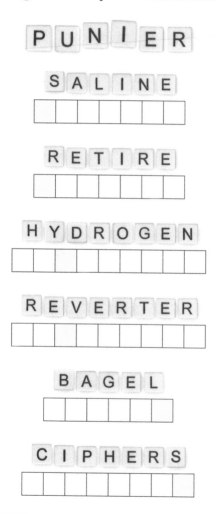

P U N I E R

S A L I N E

R E T I R E

H Y D R O G E N

R E V E R T E R

BONUS WORD

B A G E L

C I P H E R S

 **BANANA SPLITS**

For each of the three words below, change one letter to an A **and then rearrange the letters to spell a type of fish.**

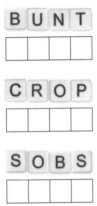

B U N T

C R O P

S O B S

For each of the three words below, change one letter to an L **and then rearrange the letters to spell a type of spice or herb.**

S W A T

I D O L

V O I C E

Replace each of the question marks below with one of the five letters V , W , Y , F **or** H **and then rearrange the letters to form a common word. Each of the five letters will be used only once.**

A C H O ?

A A E R ?

A C D N ?

A K N R ?

E M R Y ?

33

BANANA TREES

LEVEL

Use the 15 tiles in this bunch to create words that fit into the grids below. You will reuse this bunch for each of the four grids. The BANANA BITES provide hints to help you solve each grid.

E C L E C E F I
O I X D N P I

1. BANANA BITE: One word means "to perform well."

2. BANANA BITE: One word means "created a word."

3. BANANA BITE: One word is a type of animal.

4. BANANA BITE: One word is something babies get.

34

Use the 15 tiles in this bunch to create words that fit into the grids below. You will reuse this bunch for each of the four grids. The BANANA BITES provide hints to help you solve each grid.

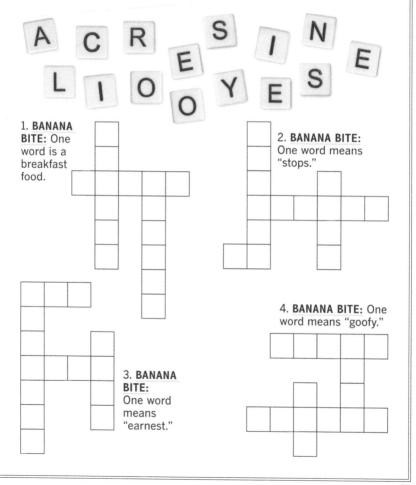

1. BANANA BITE: One word is a breakfast food.

2. BANANA BITE: One word means "stops."

3. BANANA BITE: One word means "earnest."

4. BANANA BITE: One word means "goofy."

There is <u>one letter</u> that when added to all of the four-letter words below can be used to form new five-letter words. Find the letter that works for all four words, add it to each word, and then rearrange each set of letters to form a new word. For example, L can be added to ROADS, WEARY, EPICS and GONER to form DORSAL, LAWYER, SPLICE and LONGER.

COMMON
LETTER

MULE

TINE

TOAD

NAYS

For each of the words below, replace one letter with the tile after the plus sign. Then rearrange the letters to spell the name of a U.S. state.

T H A T + U

☐ ☐ ☐ ☐

A D V E N T + A

☐ ☐ ☐ ☐ ☐ ☐

H O O K + I

☐ ☐ ☐ ☐

S A U N A S + K

☐ ☐ ☐ ☐ ☐ ☐

G O V E R N + O

☐ ☐ ☐ ☐ ☐ ☐

D A T E S + X

☐ ☐ ☐ ☐ ☐

R A D I O + H

☐ ☐ ☐ ☐ ☐

BANANA FILLING

LEVEL

Add a D **to each of the words below and then rearrange the letters in each word to form a new six-letter word.**

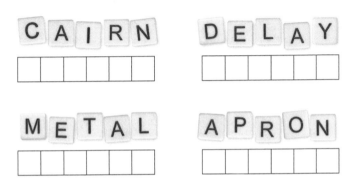

C A I R N

☐☐☐☐☐☐

D E L A Y

☐☐☐☐☐☐

M E T A L

☐☐☐☐☐☐

A P R O N

☐☐☐☐☐☐

Using any letters EXCEPT the ones that appear in the bunch below, fill in the blanks to form three new words.

E M

N P

V Y

☐☐ L I N E

☐☐ C A N E

☐☐ T R A Y

Using three of the tiles from each bunch on the left, fill in the blanks on the right to make a six-letter word that connects the grid.

BUNCH OF BANANAS

LEVEL

For each word below, rearrange the letters to spell two new words that are both kinds of creatures. For example, FLOORING becomes FROG and LION.

DONATE

☐☐☐☐   ☐☐☐

BEATER

☐☐☐☐   ☐☐☐

ACETUM

☐☐☐☐   ☐☐☐

SHOALING

☐☐☐☐☐☐   ☐☐☐

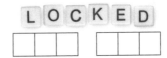

LOCKED

☐☐☐☐   ☐☐☐

Each set of 15 tiles below contains three common five-letter words. The letters of the first five-letter word are adjacent, but not in order. Find them and rearrange them to spell a word. Cross out those letters and imagine that the 10 remaining letters are now consecutive. Find five more adjacent letters that can be rearranged into the second word and then cross them out. The remaining five letters can now be rearranged to spell the final word.

Example: GANKNRNOTFHITIC. FRONT is the first word, which leaves GANKNHITIC. THINK is the second word, which leaves GANIC. That can be unscrambled into ACING.

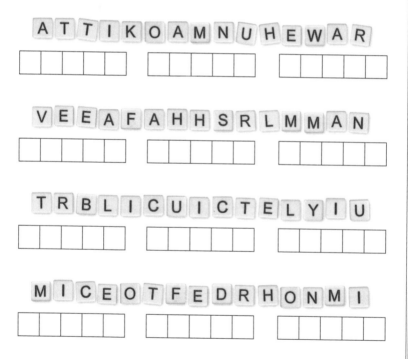

A T T I K O A M N U H E W A R

V E E A F A H H S R L M M A N

T R B L I C U I C T E L Y I U

M I C E O T F E D R H O N M I

GO BANANAS!

LEVEL

Use all 21 tiles in this bunch to create a collection of connecting and intersecting common words in the grid below. **Any word that has more than two letters must be a type of American coin.** The words may be horizontal or vertical, reading left to right or top to bottom.

Use all 21 tiles in this bunch to create a collection of connecting and intersecting common words in the grid below. **Any word that has more than two letters must be a type of music.** The words may be horizontal or vertical, reading left to right or top to bottom.

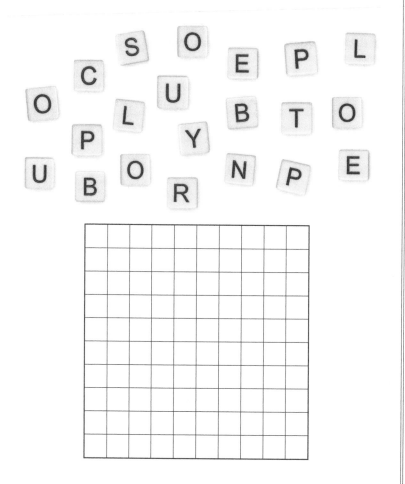

For each of the word groups below, change one letter in the top word to one of the letters that appears in the bottom word, then rearrange the tiles to form a new common word. Do the same with each new word until you arrive at the bottom word. For example, a path from BARK to PLUM is BARK, MARK, RAMP, RUMP, PLUM.

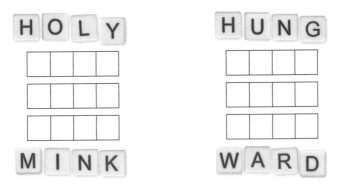

44

Each of the two-letter words below may be extended both on the right and the left to form a six-letter word. Drawing from the tiles directly above each word, fill in the blanks to find the longer words as quickly as you can.

B C D E O R T
☐ ☐ O N ☐ ☐

E G I N N T U
☐ ☐ D O ☐ ☐

B E I N O T Y
☐ ☐ G O ☐ ☐

A B I O R S U
☐ ☐ P E ☐ ☐

A E G H N O Y
☐ ☐ M A ☐ ☐

TOP BANANA

LEVEL

For each bunch below, rearrange the letters to form two intersecting words that fit into the corresponding grid.

For each of the six words below, add one letter from the word **PURRED** (each letter will be used only once) and then rearrange the letters to spell a kind of bird. Once you've filled in all the blanks, take the shaded letters from each line and rearrange them to spell a bonus bird.

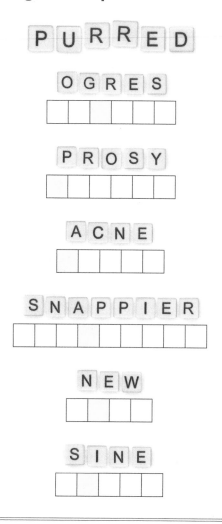

P U R R E D

O G R E S

P R O S Y

A C N E

S N A P P I E R

BONUS WORD

N E W

S I N E

47

For each of the three words below, change one letter to an A **and then rearrange the letters to spell a condition or disease.**

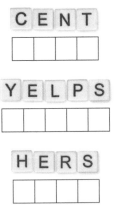

C E N T

Y E L P S

H E R S

For each of the three words below, change one letter to an O **and then rearrange the letters to spell a type of building.**

S H U T E

T U R F

W A T E R

48

Replace each of the question marks below with one of the five letters V, W, Y, F or H and then rearrange the letters to form a common word. Each of the five letters will be used only once.

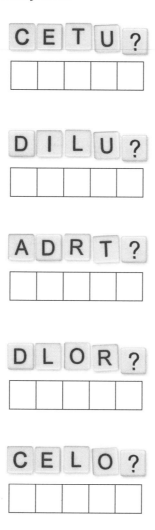

C E T U ?

D I L U ?

A D R T ?

D L O R ?

C E L O ?

49

LEVEL

Use the 15 tiles in this bunch to create words that fit into the grids below. You will reuse this bunch for each of the four grids. The BANANA BITES provide hints to help you solve each grid.

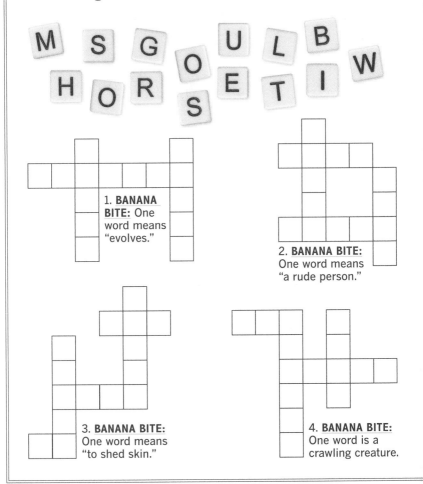

1. **BANANA BITE:** One word means "evolves."

2. **BANANA BITE:** One word means "a rude person."

3. **BANANA BITE:** One word means "to shed skin."

4. **BANANA BITE:** One word is a crawling creature.

Use the 15 tiles in this bunch to create words that fit into the grids below. You will reuse this bunch for each of the four grids. The BANANA BITES provide hints to help you solve each grid.

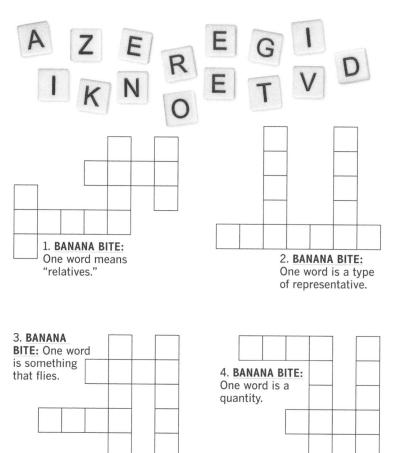

A Z E R E G I D
I K N O E T V

1. **BANANA BITE:** One word means "relatives."

2. **BANANA BITE:** One word is a type of representative.

3. **BANANA BITE:** One word is something that flies.

4. **BANANA BITE:** One word is a quantity.

There is <u>one letter</u> that when added to all of the four-letter words below can be used to form new five-letter words. Find the letter that works for all four words, add it to each word, and then rearrange each set of letters to form a new word. For example, L can be added to ROADS, WEARY, EPICS and GONER to form DORSAL, LAWYER, SPLICE and LONGER.

COMMON
LETTER

E A C H

H E W N

Y A P S

W O R D

For each of the words below, replace one letter with the tile after the plus sign. Then rearrange the letters to spell a type of clothing.

T U N A S + P

[ ] [ ] [ ] [ ] [ ]

R E A D S + S

[ ] [ ] [ ] [ ] [ ]

P I T + E

[ ] [ ] [ ] [ ]

L O D G E S + V

[ ] [ ] [ ] [ ] [ ] [ ]

C R O S S + K

[ ] [ ] [ ] [ ] [ ]

W R I S T + H

[ ] [ ] [ ] [ ] [ ]

S E A T + V

[ ] [ ] [ ] [ ]

53

BANANA FILLING

LEVEL

Add a **C** to each of the words below and then rearrange the letters in each word to form a new six-letter word.

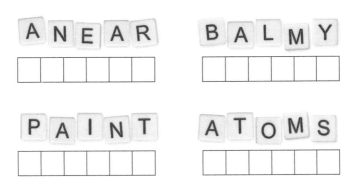

A N E A R

☐☐☐☐☐☐

B A L M Y

☐☐☐☐☐☐

P A I N T

☐☐☐☐☐☐

A T O M S

☐☐☐☐☐☐

Using any letters EXCEPT the ones that appear in the bunch below, fill in the blanks to form three new words.

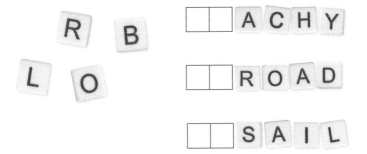

R B

L O

☐☐ A C H Y

☐☐ R O A D

☐☐ S A I L

54

Using three of the tiles from each bunch on the left, fill in the blanks on the right to make a six-letter word that connects the grid.

BUNCH OF BANANAS

LEVEL

For each word below, rearrange the letters to spell two new words that are both kinds of creatures. For example, **FLOORING** becomes **FROG** and **LION**.

56

Each set of 15 tiles below contains three common five-letter words. The letters of the first five-letter word are adjacent, but not in order. Find them and rearrange them to spell a word. Cross out those letters and imagine that the 10 remaining letters are now consecutive. Find five more adjacent letters that can be rearranged into the second word and then cross them out. The remaining five letters can now be rearranged to spell the final word.

Example: GANKNRNOTFHITIC. FRONT is the first word, which leaves GANKNHITIC. THINK is the second word, which leaves GANIC. That can be unscrambled into ACING.

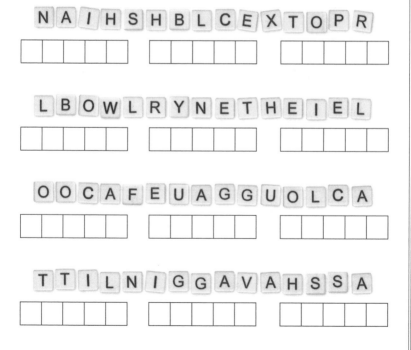

N A I H S H B L C E X T O P R

L B O W L R Y N E T H E I E L

O O C A F E U A G G U O L C A

T T I L N I G G A V A H S S A

GO BANANAS!

LEVEL

Use all 21 tiles in this bunch to create a collection of connecting and intersecting common words in the grid below. **Any word that has more than two letters must be a type of furniture.** The words may be horizontal or vertical, reading left to right or top to bottom.

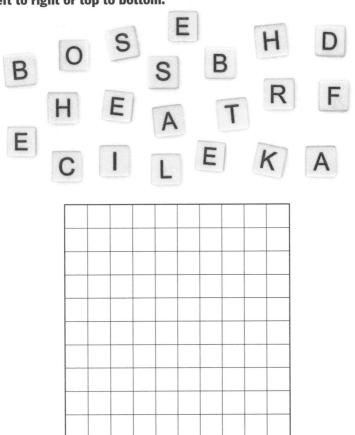

Use all 21 tiles in this bunch to create a collection of connecting and intersecting common words in the grid below. <u>Any word that has more than two letters must be a European nation.</u> The words may be horizontal or vertical, reading left to right or top to bottom.

For each of the word groups below, change one letter in the
top word to one of the letters that appears in the bottom
word, then rearrange the tiles to form a new common word.
Do the same with each new word until you arrive at the
bottom word. For example, the path from BARK to PLUM
is BARK, MARK, RAMP, RUMP, PLUM.

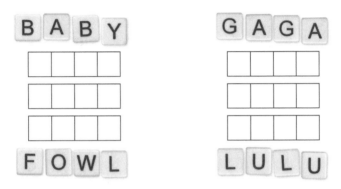

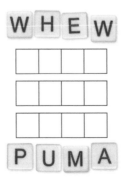

Each of the two-letter words below may be extended both on the right and the left to form a six-letter word. Drawing from the tiles directly above each word, fill in the blanks to find the longer words as quickly as you can.

A F F I L R U

☐ ☐ N O ☐ ☐

A E F H L S T

☐ ☐ W E ☐ ☐

C E G M N O S

☐ ☐ L A ☐ ☐

A C F I K L T

☐ ☐ L I ☐ ☐

A D I M N R T

☐ ☐ H I ☐ ☐

LEVEL

For each bunch below, rearrange the letters to form two intersecting words that fit into the corresponding grid.

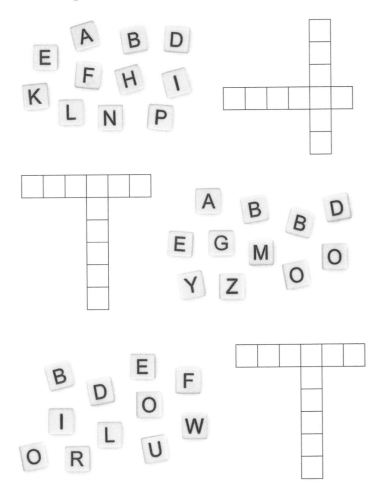

For each of the six words below, add one letter from the word **MALIGN** (each letter will be used only once) and then rearrange the letters to spell a kind of fish. Once you've filled in all the blanks, take the shaded letters from each line and rearrange them to spell a bonus fish.

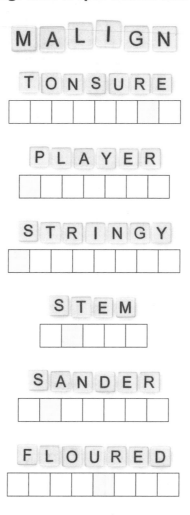

M A L I G N

T O N S U R E

P L A Y E R

S T R I N G Y

S T E M

S A N D E R

BONUS WORD

F L O U R E D

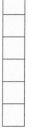

For each of the three words below, change one letter to an [I] and then rearrange the letters to spell a word of Japanese origin.

B A R O N S

D A I K O N

G A S H E S

For each of the three words below, change one letter to an [A] and then rearrange the letters to spell a word of Spanish origin.

M I S D O

C H O M P

U M B E R

Replace each of the question marks below with one of the five letters V, W, Y, F or H **and then rearrange the letters to form a common word. Each of the five letters will be used only once.**

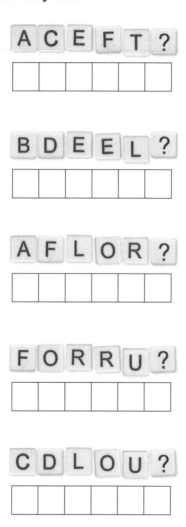

A C E F T ?

B D E E L ?

A F L O R ?

F O R R U ?

C D L O U ?

Use the 15 tiles in this bunch to fill in each of the four grids below. To get you started, a few tiles from the bunch have been placed in each grid. Using the remaining tiles in the bunch, find words that complete each grid.

Use the 15 tiles in this bunch to fill in each of the four grids below. To get you started, a few tiles from the bunch have been placed in each grid. Using the remaining tiles in the bunch, find words that complete each grid.

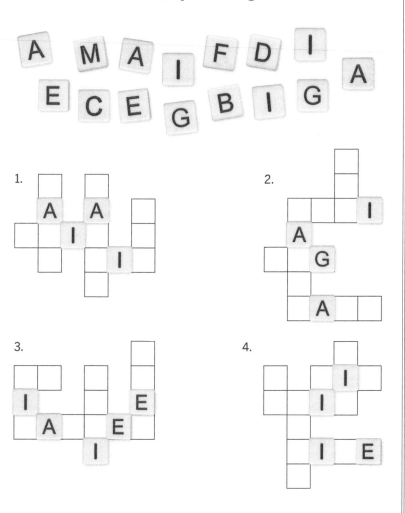

There is <u>one letter</u> that when added to all of the five-letter words below can be used to form new six-letter words. Find the letter that works for all four words, add it to each word, and then rearrange each set of letters to form a new word. For example, L can be added to ROADS, WEARY, EPICS and GONER to form DORSAL, LAWYER, SPLICE and LONGER.

COMMON
LETTER

⬜

| V | O | T | E | R |

| | | | | | |

| T | H | E | M | E |

| | | | | | |

| A | U | N | T | S |

| | | | | | |

| M | E | A | T | Y |

| | | | | | |

For each of the words below, replace one letter with the tile after the plus sign. Then rearrange the letters to spell a word related to baseball.

M E R I T S + K

[ ][ ][ ][ ][ ][ ]

T R I C E P S + H

[ ][ ][ ][ ][ ][ ][ ]

R O M E O + H

[ ][ ][ ][ ][ ]

A V E N G E R + A

[ ][ ][ ][ ][ ][ ][ ]

A L T E R + S

[ ][ ][ ][ ][ ][ ]

P R E L I M + U

[ ][ ][ ][ ][ ][ ]

S E D A N S + T

[ ][ ][ ][ ][ ][ ]

BANANA FILLING

LEVEL

Add a G **to each of the words below and then rearrange the letters in each word to form a new seven-letter word.**

L O C A L E

D E A D E R

L E A S E S

S T O L E N

Using any letters EXCEPT the ones that appear in the bunch below, fill in the blanks to form three new words.

D I S T I C N H L U

☐ ☐ A G I L E

☐ ☐ A P I N G

☐ ☐ A M I N E

Using four of the tiles from each bunch on the left, fill in the blanks on the right to make a seven-letter word that connects the grid.

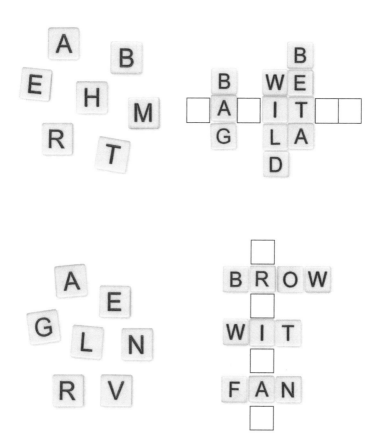

BUNCH OF BANANAS

LEVEL

For each word below, rearrange the letters to spell two new words that are both kinds of food. For example, TRAPEZII becomes ZITI and PEAR.

Each set of 15 tiles below contains three common five-letter words. The letters of the first five-letter word are adjacent, but not in order. Find them and rearrange them to spell a word. Cross out those letters and imagine that the 10 remaining letters are now consecutive. Find five more adjacent letters that can be rearranged into the second word and then cross them out. The remaining five letters can now be rearranged to spell the final word.

Example: GANKNRNOTFHITIC. FRONT is the first word, which leaves GANKNHITIC. THINK is the second word, which leaves GANIC. That can be unscrambled into ACING.

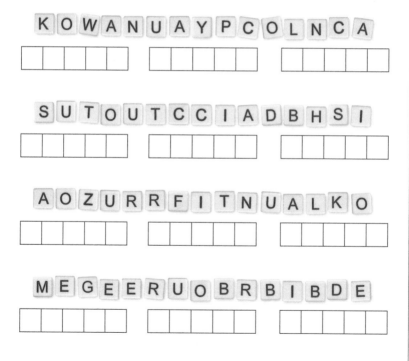

K O W A N U A Y P C O L N C A

S U T O U T C C I A D B H S I

A O Z U R R F I T N U A L K O

M E G E E R U O B R B I B D E

GO BANANAS!

LEVEL

Use all 21 tiles in this bunch to create a collection of connecting and intersecting common words in the grid below. **Any word longer than two letters must be a five-letter word that has an R as its 2nd and 5th letter.** The words may be horizontal or vertical, reading left to right or top to bottom.

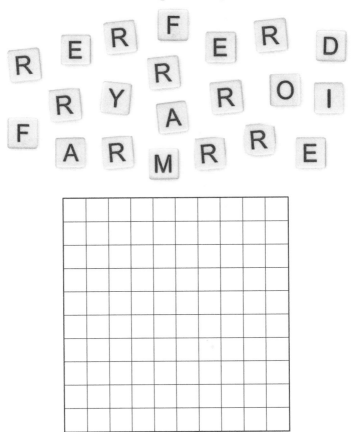

Use all 21 tiles in this bunch to create a collection of connecting and intersecting common words in the grid below. **Any word longer than two letters must be a five-letter word that begins and ends with an A.** The words may be horizontal or vertical, reading left to right or top to bottom.

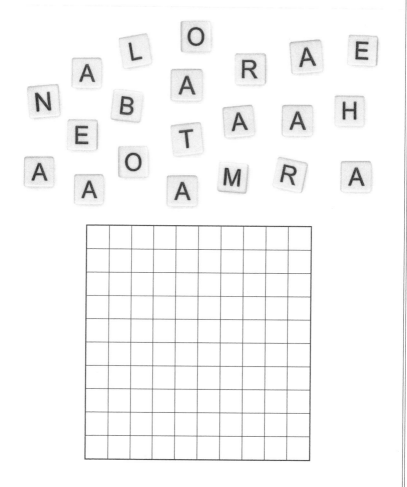

For each of the word groups below, change one letter in the top word to one of the letters that appears in the bottom word, then rearrange the tiles to form a new common word. Do the same with each new word until you arrive at the bottom word. For example, a path from **BARK** to **PLUM** is **BARK, MARK, RAMP, RUMP, PLUM.**

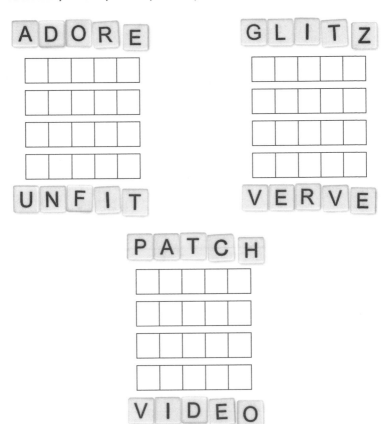

Each of the three-letter words below may be extended both on the right and the left to form a seven-letter word. Drawing from the tiles directly above each word, fill in the blanks to find the longer words as quickly as you can.

C E E L M O R

☐ ☐ A N D ☐ ☐

C E E O P R S

☐ ☐ L I P ☐ ☐

A B G L M R U

☐ ☐ E N D ☐ ☐

D E I M O P Y

☐ ☐ R A M ☐ ☐

B I N O S S T

☐ ☐ O N E ☐ ☐

TOP BANANA

LEVEL

For each bunch below, rearrange the letters to form two intersecting words that fit into the corresponding grid.

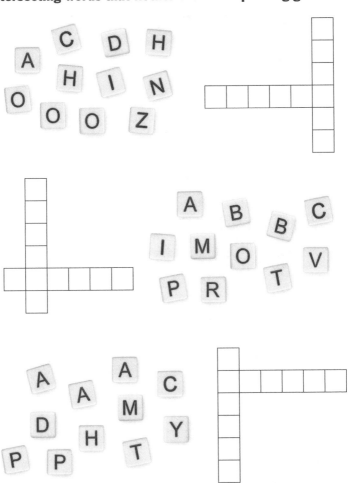

For each of the six words below, add one letter from the word **BUNGLE** (each letter will be used only once) and then rearrange the letters to spell a part of the body. Once you've filled in all the blanks, take the shaded letters from each line and rearrange them to spell a bonus body part.

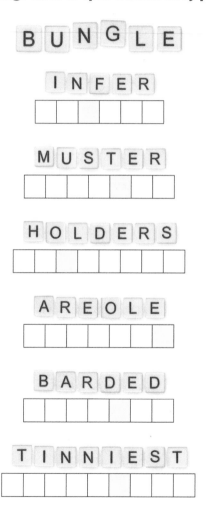

B U N G L E

I N F E R

M U S T E R

H O L D E R S

A R E O L E

B A R D E D

T I N N I E S T

BONUS WORD

LEVEL

For each of the three words below, change one letter to an E and then rearrange the letters to spell a word of French origin.

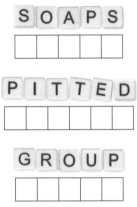

S O A P S

☐ ☐ ☐ ☐ ☐

P I T T E D

☐ ☐ ☐ ☐ ☐ ☐

G R O U P

☐ ☐ ☐ ☐ ☐

For each of the three words below, change one letter to an E and then rearrange the letters to spell a type of mood or emotion.

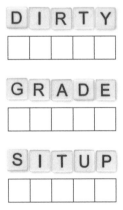

D I R T Y

☐ ☐ ☐ ☐ ☐

G R A D E

☐ ☐ ☐ ☐ ☐

S I T U P

☐ ☐ ☐ ☐ ☐

Replace each of the question marks below with one of the five letters V, W, Y, F or H and then rearrange the letters to form a common word. Each of the five letters will be used only once.

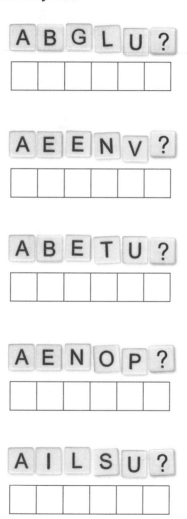

A B G L U ?

A E E N V ?

A B E T U ?

A E N O P ?

A I L S U ?

BANANA TREES

LEVEL

Use the 15 tiles in this bunch to fill in each of the four grids below. To get you started, a few tiles from the bunch have been placed in each grid. Using the remaining tiles in the bunch, find words that complete each grid.

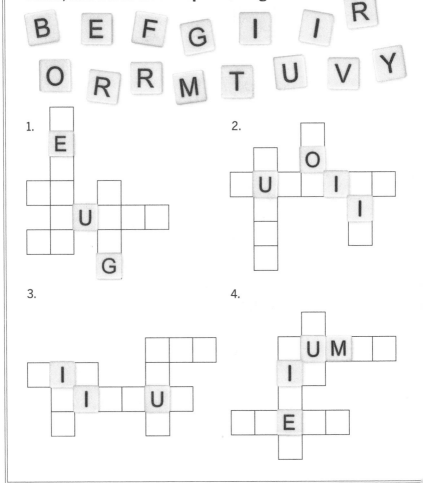

1.

2.

3.

4.

Use the 15 tiles in this bunch to fill in each of the four grids below. To get you started, a few tiles from the bunch have been placed in each grid. Using the remaining tiles in the bunch, find words that complete each grid.

1.

2.

3.

4.

There is <u>one letter</u> that when added to all of the five-letter words below can be used to form new six-letter words. Find the letter that works for all four words, add it to each word, and then rearrange each set of letters to form a new word. For example, L can be added to ROADS, WEARY, EPICS and GONER to form DORSAL, LAWYER, SPLICE and LONGER.

COMMON
LETTER

A L O N G

S U E D E

A R I A S

U L T R A

For each of the words below, replace one letter with the tile after the plus sign. Then rearrange the letters to spell a type of animal.

R I D G E + T

L O A D E R S + P

L O G I C A L + R

A C O R N + B

H E P T A N E S + L

Y E O M A N + K

I R O N Y + H

BANANA FILLING

LEVEL

Add an **L** to each of the words below and then rearrange the letters in each word to form a new seven-letter word.

P A L A T E

☐ ☐ ☐ ☐ ☐ ☐ ☐

R E C A N T

☐ ☐ ☐ ☐ ☐ ☐ ☐

B A S A L T

☐ ☐ ☐ ☐ ☐ ☐ ☐

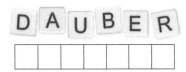

D A U B E R

☐ ☐ ☐ ☐ ☐ ☐ ☐

Using any letters EXCEPT the ones that appear in the bunch below, fill in the blanks to form three new words.

☐ ☐ C R E E D

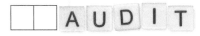

☐ ☐ A U D I T

☐ ☐ A L L O W

86

Using four of the tiles from each bunch on the left, fill in the blanks on the right to make a seven-letter word that connects the grid.

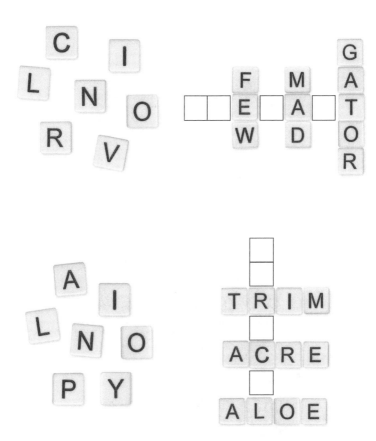

BUNCH OF BANANAS

LEVEL

For each word or phrase below, rearrange the letters to spell two new words that are both kinds of foods or drinks. For example, TRAPEZII becomes ZITI and PEAR.

WAVELETS

LIMERICK

CAPSULATE

GOOD ARENAS

APOSTATE

Each set of 15 tiles below contains three common five-letter words. The letters of the first five-letter word are adjacent, but not in order. Find them and rearrange them to spell a word. Cross out those letters and imagine that the 10 remaining letters are now consecutive. Find five more adjacent letters that can be rearranged into the second word and then cross them out. The remaining five letters can now be rearranged to spell the final word.

Example: GANKNRNOTFHITIC. FRONT is the first word, which leaves GANKNHITIC. THINK is the second word, which leaves GANIC. That can be unscrambled into ACING.

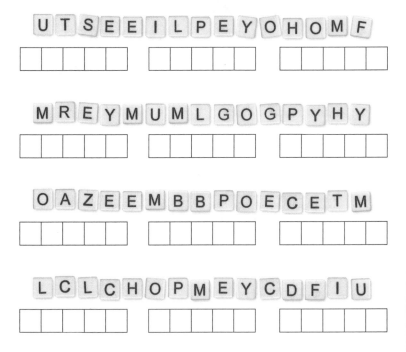

U T S E E I L P E Y O H O M F

M R E Y M U M L G O G P Y H Y

O A Z E E M B B P O E C E T M

L C L C H O P M E Y C D F I U

GO BANANAS!

LEVEL

Use all 21 tiles in this bunch to create a collection of connecting and intersecting common words in the grid below. **Any word longer than two letters must be a five-letter word that begins and ends with an L.** The words may be horizontal or vertical, reading left to right or top to bottom.

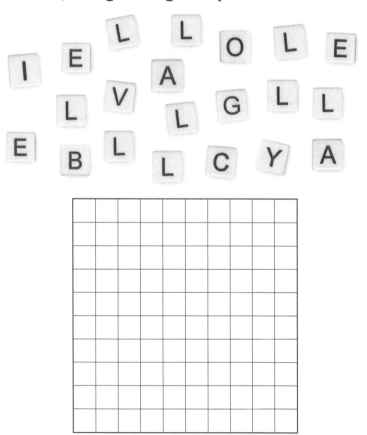

Use all 21 tiles in this bunch to create a collection of connecting and intersecting common words in the grid below. **Any word longer than two letters must be a five-letter word that has two O's, and three of these five-letter words must end in O.** The words may be horizontal or vertical, reading left to right or top to bottom.

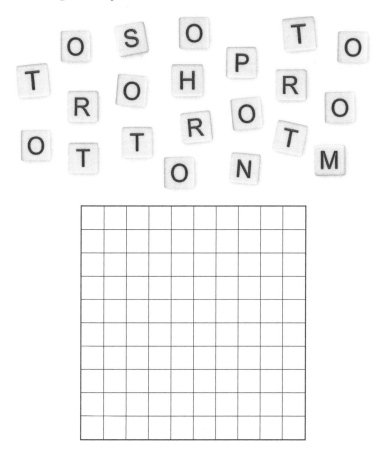

For each of the word groups below, change one letter in the top word to one of the letters that appears in the bottom word, then rearrange the tiles to form a new common word. Do the same with each new word until you arrive at the bottom word. For example, a path from BARK to PLUM is BARK, MARK, RAMP, RUMP, PLUM.

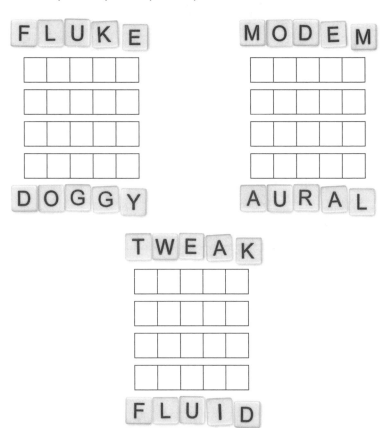

Each of the three-letter words below may be extended both on the right and the left to form a seven-letter word. Drawing from the tiles directly above each word, fill in the blanks to find the longer words as quickly as you can.

E N O P S T U

☐ ☐ A R T ☐ ☐

A A C D D N T

☐ ☐ D E N ☐ ☐

E I K N O T Y

☐ ☐ L O T ☐ ☐

E L M O P S Y

☐ ☐ P R O ☐ ☐

B D E M O O T

☐ ☐ R E D ☐ ☐

For each bunch below, rearrange the letters to form two intersecting words that fit into the corresponding grid.

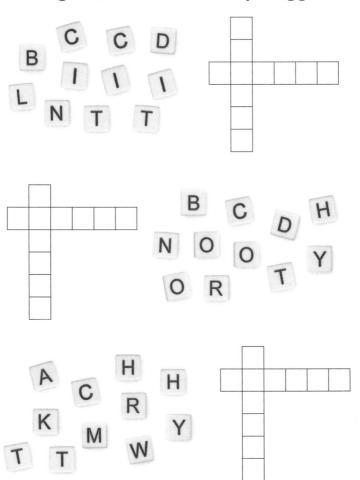

For each of the six words below, add one letter from the word CARTEL (each letter will be used only once) and then rearrange the letters to spell a kind of sport or game. Once you've filled in all the blanks, take the shaded letters from each line and rearrange them to spell a bonus sport or game.

C A R T E L

P O R K

S K I

G R A I N

F O G

BONUS
WORD

S H A R E

C H E R R Y

95

 BANANA SPLITS

LEVEL

For each of the three words below, change one letter to an $\boxed{A}$ and then rearrange the letters to spell a condition or disease.

E N R I C H

⬜⬜⬜⬜⬜⬜

B R I D E S

⬜⬜⬜⬜⬜⬜

G U L P E R

⬜⬜⬜⬜⬜⬜

For each of the three words below, change one letter to a $\boxed{U}$ and then rearrange the letters to spell a part of an animal's body.

D R E A D

⬜⬜⬜⬜⬜

O N S E T

⬜⬜⬜⬜⬜

E P O C H

⬜⬜⬜⬜⬜

Replace each of the question marks below with one of the five letters V, W, Y, F or H and then rearrange the letters to form a common word. Each of the five letters will be used only once.

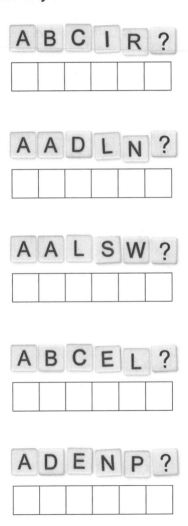

A B C I R ?

A A D L N ?

A A L S W ?

A B C E L ?

A D E N P ?

BANANA TREES

LEVEL

Use the 15 tiles in this bunch to fill in each of the four grids below. To get you started, a few tiles from the bunch have been placed in each grid. Using the remaining tiles in the bunch, find words that complete each grid.

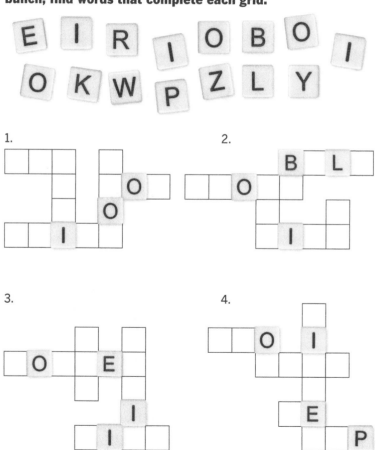

Use the 15 tiles in this bunch to fill in each of the four grids below. To get you started, a few tiles from the bunch have been placed in each grid. Using the remaining tiles in the bunch, find words that complete each grid.

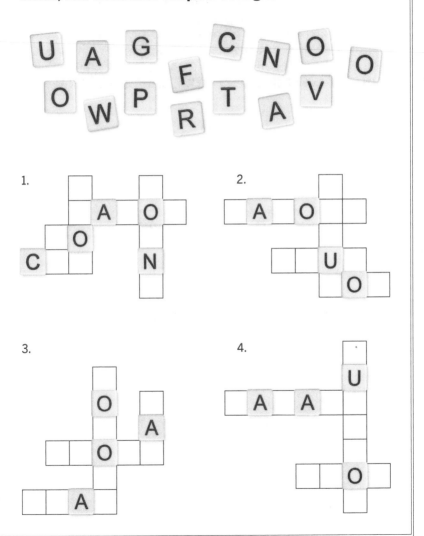

BANANA PEELS

LEVEL

There is <u>one letter</u> that when added to all of the five-letter words below can be used to form new six-letter words. Find the letter that works for all four words, add it to each word, and then rearrange each set of letters to form a new word. For example, L can be added to ROADS, WEARY, EPICS and GONER to form DORSAL, LAWYER, SPLICE and LONGER.

COMMON
LETTER

☐

H O U R S

A V A S T

V O I C E

F A I N T

For each of the words below, replace one letter with the tile after the plus sign. Then rearrange the letters to spell a type of household appliance.

P E O N Y + H

L E A R N E D + B

P O E T S + V

F A I R E D + G

R E A D Y + R

D R A I N + O

S P E C T R U M + O

BANANA FILLING

LEVEL

Add an M to each of the words below and then rearrange the letters in each word to form a new seven-letter word.

R A D I A L

A U D I T S

I T C H E S

O U N C E S

Using any letters EXCEPT the ones that appear in the bunch below, fill in the blanks to form three new words.

C F P N X O T D

☐ ☐ A S T E R

☐ ☐ A C T O R

☐ ☐ A S I D E

Using four of the tiles from each bunch on the left, fill in the blanks on the right to make a seven-letter word that connects the grid.

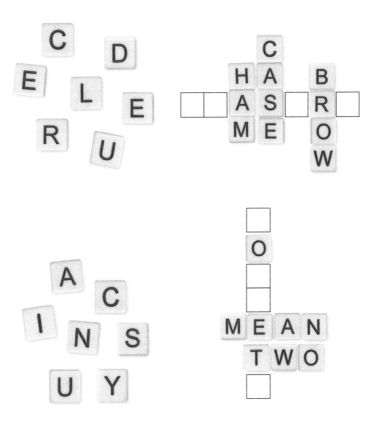

BUNCH OF BANANAS

For each phrase below, rearrange the letters to spell two new words that are both kinds of food. For example, TRAPEZII becomes ZITI and PEAR.

HONES FILM

☐☐☐☐☐ ☐☐☐☐☐

US ENGAGED

☐☐☐☐ ☐☐☐☐☐☐

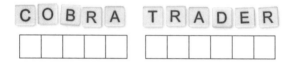

COBRA TRADER

☐☐☐☐☐☐ ☐☐☐☐☐☐

PLAYPEN CAD

☐☐☐☐☐☐ ☐☐☐☐☐

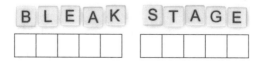

BLEAK STAGE

☐☐☐☐☐ ☐☐☐☐☐

Each set of 15 tiles below contains three common five-letter words. The letters of the first five-letter word are adjacent, but not in order. Find them and rearrange them to spell a word. Cross out those letters and imagine that the 10 remaining letters are now consecutive. Find five more adjacent letters that can be rearranged into the second word and then cross them out. The remaining five letters can now be rearranged to spell the final word.

Example: GANKNRNOTFHITIC. FRONT is the first word, which leaves GANKNHITIC. THINK is the second word, which leaves GANIC. That can be unscrambled into ACING.

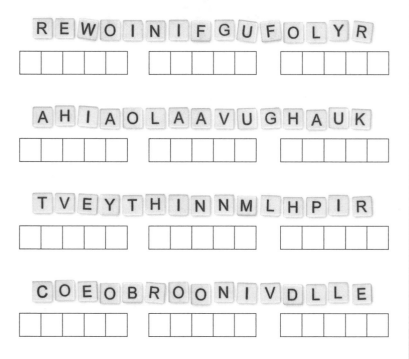

R E W O I N I F G U F O L Y R

A H I A O L A A V U G H A U K

T V E Y T H I N N M L H P I R

C O E O B R O O N I V D L L E

GO BANANAS!

LEVEL

Use all 21 tiles in this bunch to create a collection of connecting and intersecting common words in the grid below. **Any word longer than two letters must be a five-letter word that has two I's.** The words may be horizontal or vertical, reading left to right or top to bottom.

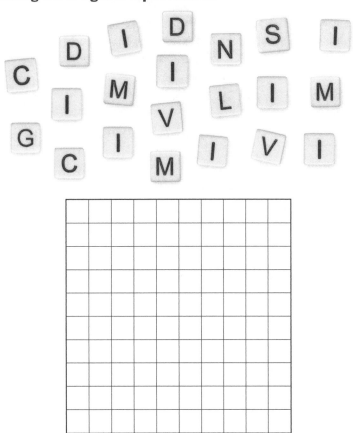

Use all 21 tiles in this bunch to create a collection of
connecting and intersecting common words in the grid below.
<u>Any word longer than two letters must be a five-letter word
that has two T's.</u> The words may be horizontal or vertical,
reading left to right or top to bottom.

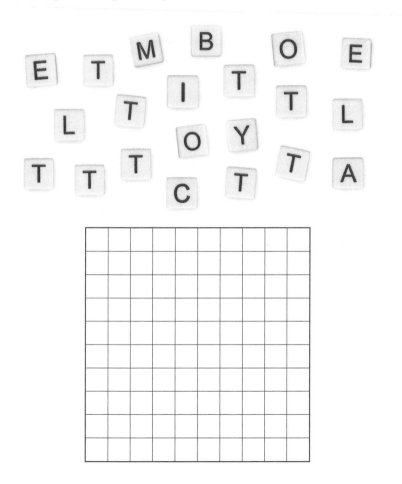

For each of the word groups below, change one letter in the top word to one of the letters that appears in the bottom word, then rearrange the tiles to form a new common word. Do the same with each new word until you arrive at the bottom word. For example, the path from **BARK** to **PLUM** is **BARK, MARK, RAMP, RUMP, PLUM.**

M A G I C

☐☐☐☐☐

☐☐☐☐☐

☐☐☐☐☐

☐☐☐☐☐

W O U L D

C L I P T

☐☐☐☐☐

☐☐☐☐☐

☐☐☐☐☐

☐☐☐☐☐

B R O W N

C O O P T

☐☐☐☐☐

☐☐☐☐☐

☐☐☐☐☐

☐☐☐☐☐

R H Y M E

Each of the three-letter words below may be extended both on the right and the left to form a seven-letter word. Drawing from the tiles directly above each word, fill in the blanks to find the longer words as quickly as you can.

I L N O O R U
☐ ☐ C A T ☐ ☐

C H I N O T U
☐ ☐ M A D ☐ ☐

C E H I N R U
☐ ☐ H I T ☐ ☐

B E E N O T V
☐ ☐ L I E ☐ ☐

C E H I I L T
☐ ☐ T A D ☐ ☐

LEVEL

For each bunch below, rearrange the letters to form two intersecting words that fit into the corresponding grid.

For each of the six words below, add one letter from the word BAMBOO (each letter will be used only once) and then rearrange the letters to spell a major city. Once you've filled in all the blanks, take the shaded letters from each line and rearrange them to spell a bonus city.

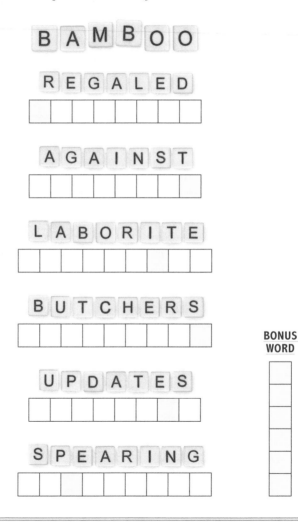

B A M B O O

R E G A L E D

A G A I N S T

L A B O R I T E

B U T C H E R S

U P D A T E S

S P E A R I N G

BONUS WORD

LEVEL

For each of the three words below, change one letter to an I and then rearrange the letters to spell a word of Italian origin.

ALARMS

□□□□□□

NARCOMAS

□□□□□□□□

CANOES

□□□□□□

For each of the three words below, change one letter to an A and then rearrange the letters to spell a type of mood or emotion.

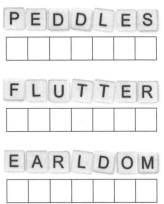

PEDDLES

□□□□□□□

FLUTTER

□□□□□□□

EARLDOM

□□□□□□□

112

Replace each of the question marks below with one of the five letters V, W, Y, F or H and then rearrange the letters to form a common word. Each of the five letters will be used only once.

A A D I R ?

A A L M N ?

A E G O Y ?

A B I N S ?

A A H S S ?

BANANA TREES

LEVEL

Use the 18 tiles in this bunch to fill in each of the three grids below. To get you started, a few tiles from the bunch have been placed in each grid, and the BANANA BITES provide hints. Using the remaining tiles in the bunch, find words that complete each grid.

A T F U O D
H E R D T S N
N R E T A

O U
E D

1. BANANA BITE: One word is something that can be told.

R A

2. BANANA BITE: One word means "sun-browned."

N
E U E

A D
U
A

3. BANANA BITE: One word means "make stronger."

O E N

Use the 18 tiles in this bunch to fill in each of the three grids below. To get you started, a few tiles from the bunch have been placed in each grid, and the BANANA BITES provide hints. Using the remaining tiles in the bunch, find words that complete each grid.

1. **BANANA BITE:** One word means "a state of ecstasy."

2. **BANANA BITE:** One word means "urge."

3. **BANANA BITE:** One word is a type of dessert.

LEVEL

There is <u>one letter</u> that when added to all of the six-letter words below can be used to form new seven-letter words. Find the letter that works for all four words, add it to each word, and then rearrange each set of letters to form a new word. For example, L can be added to ROADS, WEARY, EPICS and GONER to form DORSAL, LAWYER, SPLICE and LONGER.

COMMON
LETTER

KARATE

LARIAT

BOATER

SOWERS

For each of the words below, replace one letter with the tile after the plus sign. Then rearrange the letters to spell the name of a profession.

R E S E E I N G + N

O B L I G A T O S + I

C O R P O R A T E S + U

R H E T O R I C + D

A R S E N A L S + M

R E S O U N D + G

O U T R A N + H

BANANA FILLING

LEVEL

Add an N to each of the words below and then rearrange the letters in each word to form a new seven-letter word.

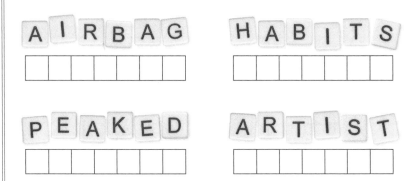

A I R B A G

| | | | | | | |

H A B I T S

| | | | | | | |

P E A K E D

| | | | | | | |

A R T I S T

| | | | | | | |

Using any letters EXCEPT the ones that appear in the bunch below, fill in the blanks to form three new words.

B E I M U

| | R A T I N G

| | R A N G E D

| | E N A B L E

Using five of the tiles from each bunch on the left, fill in the blanks on the right to make an eight-letter word that connects the grid.

BUNCH OF BANANAS

LEVEL

For each phrase below, rearrange the letters to spell two new words that are both kinds of plants or flowers. For example, A SASSY GRID becomes DAISY and GRASS.

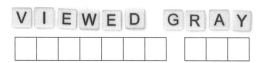

VIEWED GRAY

MAIL CUTUPS

BAN HOAGIES

MY LOYAL CRIES

BASSOON IRE

Each set of letters below is arranged alphabetically, and the
? is in the correct alphabetical position. Figure out what
letter the ? represents and rearrange the letters to spell a
six-letter word. For example, in DL?PRUY the ? could be an
L, M, N, O or P. Here it represents an O, which can be
combined with the other letters to spell PROUDLY.

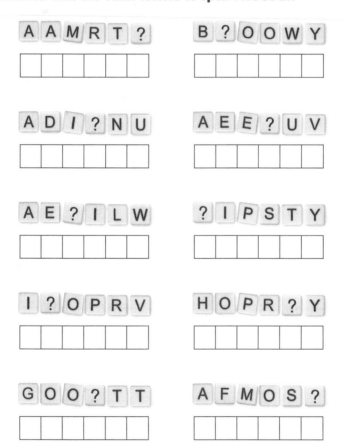

A A M R T ?

| | | | | | |

B ? O O W Y

| | | | | | |

A D I ? N U

| | | | | | |

A E E ? U V

| | | | | | |

A E ? I L W

| | | | | | |

? I P S T Y

| | | | | | |

I ? O P R V

| | | | | | |

H O P R ? Y

| | | | | | |

G O O ? T T

| | | | | | |

A F M O S ?

| | | | | | |

GO BANANAS!

LEVEL

Use all 21 tiles in this bunch to create a collection of exactly four connecting and intersecting common words in the grid below. **All four of the words must begin with the same letter.** The words may be horizontal or vertical, reading left to right or top to bottom.

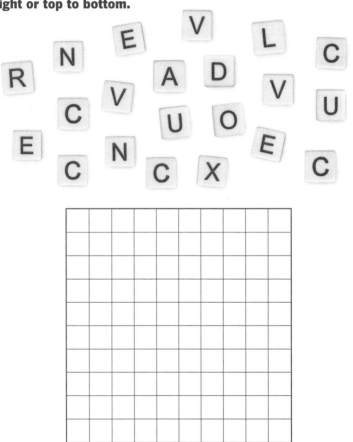

Use all 21 tiles in this bunch to create a collection of exactly four connecting and intersecting common words in the grid below. **All four of the words must begin with the same letter.** The words may be horizontal or vertical, reading left to right or top to bottom.

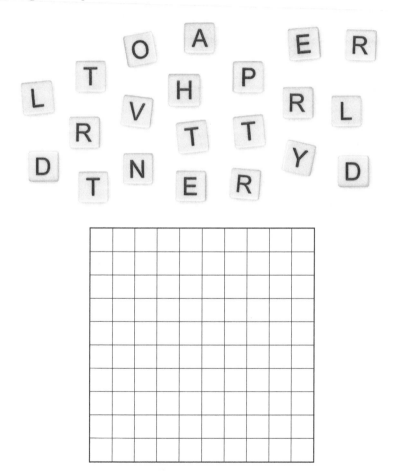

BANANA BOATS

For both of the word groups below, change one letter in the top word to one of the letters that appears in the bottom word, then rearrange the tiles to form a new common word. Do the same with each new word until you arrive at the bottom word. For example, a path from BARK to PLUM is BARK, MARK, RAMP, RUMP, PLUM.

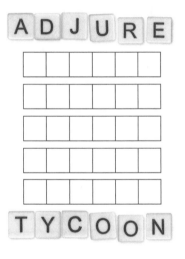

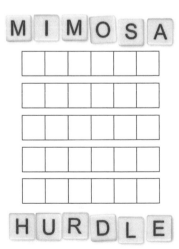

Each of the four-letter words below may be extended both on the right and the left to form an eight-letter word. Drawing from the tiles directly above each word, fill in the blanks to find the longer words as quickly as you can.

C E L M S T Y
☐ ☐ A G E R ☐ ☐

A A E I N P Y
☐ ☐ S L E W ☐ ☐

C E I L R S V
☐ ☐ B R A N ☐ ☐

A I L N O P T
☐ ☐ B L E T ☐ ☐

C E I L M R S
☐ ☐ P H A T ☐ ☐

For each bunch below, rearrange the letters to form two intersecting words that fit into the corresponding grid.

For each of the six words below, add one letter from the word LATHES (each letter will be used only once) and then rearrange the letters to spell a kind of transportation. Once you've filled in all the blanks, take the shaded letters from each line and rearrange them to spell a bonus form of transport.

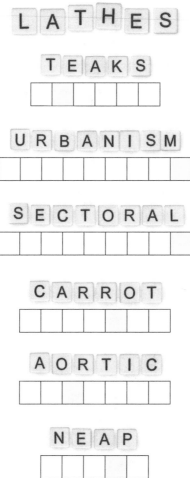

L A T H E S

T E A K S

U R B A N I S M

S E C T O R A L

C A R R O T

A O R T I C

N E A P

BONUS WORD

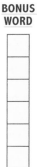

BANANA SPLITS

LEVEL

For each of the three words below, change one letter to an [L] and then rearrange the letters to spell a word related to the military.

C O N S O L E

☐☐☐☐☐☐☐

B A R M A I D

☐☐☐☐☐☐☐

S A N T E R A

☐☐☐☐☐☐☐

For each of the three words below, change one letter to an [R] and then rearrange the letters to spell a part of an animal's body.

S O L F E G E

☐☐☐☐☐☐☐

E N T A I L

☐☐☐☐☐☐

G L I S T E N

☐☐☐☐☐☐☐

Replace each of the question marks below with one of the five letters V, W, Y, F or H and then rearrange the letters to form a common word. Each of the five letters will be used only once.

C E R U W ?

B I R S U ?

A L R S U ?

A O O R R ?

A I I R T ?

Use the 18 tiles in this bunch to fill in each of the three grids below. To get you started, a few tiles from the bunch have been placed in each grid, and the BANANA BITES provide hints. Using the remaining tiles in the bunch, find words that complete each grid.

1. **BANANA BITE:** One word is an element.

2. **BANANA BITE:** One word is a type of garment.

3. **BANANA BITE:** One word is a season.

Use the 18 tiles in this bunch to fill in each of the three grids below. To get you started, a few tiles from the bunch have been placed in each grid, and the BANANA BITES provide hints. Using the remaining tiles in the bunch, find words that complete each grid.

1. **BANANA BITE:** One word means "quickly."

2. **BANANA BITE:** One word is something you're served.

3. **BANANA BITE:** One word is an element.

BANANA PEELS

LEVEL

There is <u>one letter</u> that when added to all of the six-letter words below can be used to form new seven-letter words. Find the letter that works for all four words, add it to each word, and then rearrange each set of letters to form a new word. For example, L can be added to ROADS, WEARY, EPICS and GONER to form DORSAL, LAWYER, SPLICE and LONGER.

COMMON LETTER

R E T A C K

⬚⬚⬚⬚⬚⬚⬚

H O T T E R

⬚⬚⬚⬚⬚⬚⬚

L A U D E R

⬚⬚⬚⬚⬚⬚⬚

E D D I E S

⬚⬚⬚⬚⬚⬚⬚

132

For each of the words below, replace one letter with the tile after the plus sign. Then rearrange the letters to spell the name of a city.

P A U S E R + G

□□□□□□

I N S A N E + V

□□□□□□

B A N Y A N + L

□□□□□□

N U P T I A L S + B

□□□□□□□□

M A X I M + I

□□□□□

R A T I O + C

□□□□□

R A I N B O W + I

□□□□□□□

Add a P **to each of the words below and then rearrange the letters in each word to form a new seven-letter word.**

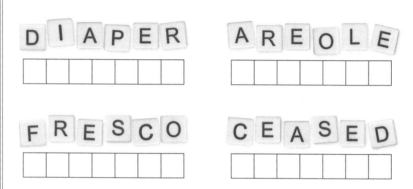

D I A P E R

A R E O L E

F R E S C O

C E A S E D

Using any letters EXCEPT the ones that appear in the bunch below, fill in the blanks to form three new words.

E G I S T

_ _ D A T I N G

_ _ A N G L E D

_ _ R A T I O N

Using five of the tiles from each bunch on the left, fill in the blanks on the right to make an eight-letter word that connects the grid.

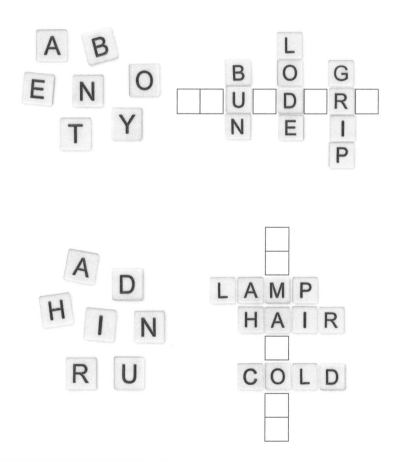

BUNCH OF BANANAS

LEVEL

For each phrase below, rearrange the letters to spell two new words that are both jobs people have. For example, I, A WORM, CYCLE becomes COMIC and LAWYER.

FOR RAT CREAM

I CREATED HAM

MORTAL BUYER

COTTON GRADE

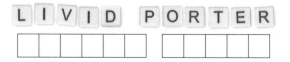

LIVID PORTER

Each set of letters below is arranged alphabetically, and the ? is in the correct alphabetical position. Figure out what letter the ? represents and rearrange the letters to spell a six-letter word. For example, in DL?PRUY the ? could be an L, M, N, O or P. Here it represents an O, which can be combined with the other letters to spell PROUDLY.

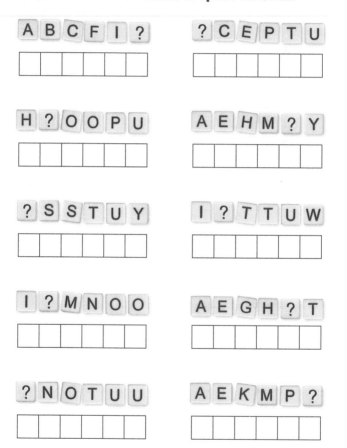

A B C F I ?

? C E P T U

H ? O O P U

A E H M ? Y

? S S T U Y

I ? T T U W

I ? M N O O

A E G H ? T

? N O T U U

A E K M P ?

GO BANANAS!

LEVEL

Use all 21 tiles in this bunch to create a collection of exactly four connecting and intersecting common words in the grid below. **All four of the words must begin with the same letter.** The words may be horizontal or vertical, reading left to right or top to bottom.

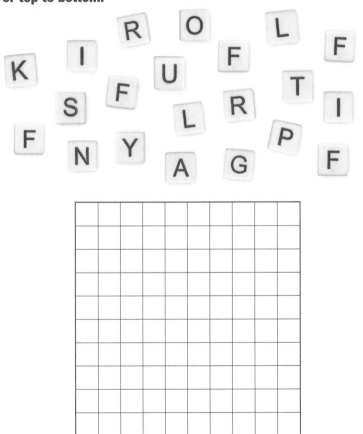

Use all 21 tiles in this bunch to create a collection of exactly four connecting and intersecting common words in the grid below. **All four of the words must begin with the same letter.** The words may be horizontal or vertical, reading left to right or top to bottom.

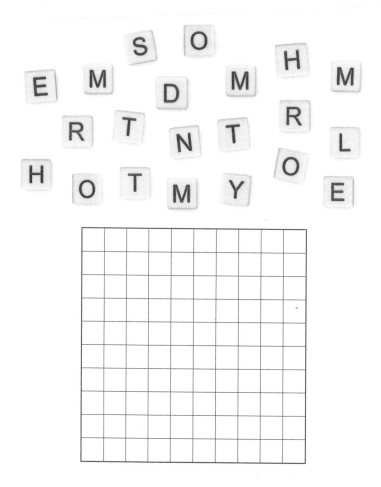

For both of the word groups below, change one letter in the top word to one of the letters that appears in the bottom word, then rearrange the tiles to form a new common word. Do the same with each new word until you arrive at the bottom word. For example, a path from BARK to PLUM is BARK, MARK, RAMP, RUMP, PLUM.

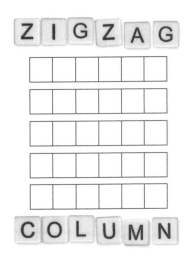

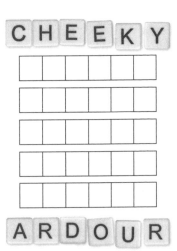

Each of the four-letter words below may be extended both on the right and the left to form an eight-letter word. Drawing from the tiles directly above each word, fill in the blanks to find the longer words as quickly as you can.

A H M O R S S

☐ ☐ L I N E ☐ ☐

A I L M O R S

☐ ☐ C H A I ☐ ☐

B E G I L M O

☐ ☐ S L A B ☐ ☐

A C E I L M R

☐ ☐ T A L L ☐ ☐

E O P R S T Y

☐ ☐ C A M O ☐ ☐

For each bunch below, rearrange the letters to form two intersecting words that fit into the corresponding grid.

For each of the six words below, add one letter from the word **HOLIER** (each letter will be used only once) and then rearrange the letters to spell a kind of musical instrument. Once you've filled in all the blanks, take the shaded letters from each line and rearrange them to spell a bonus instrument.

H O L I E R

C E N T R A L

G R A N I T E

W H I L S T

C H A I R M A N

BONUS WORD

M U D

N O R

LEVEL

For each of the three words below, change one letter to an  **E** and then rearrange the letters to spell a type of building.

R	H	I	N	O	S

C	U	T	L	A	S

C	A	R	P	A	L

For each of the three words below, change one letter to a **T** and then rearrange the letters to spell a word of Middle Eastern origin.

H	A	I	R	C	A	P

U	N	S	E	A	L

S	E	A	M	I	E	R

Replace each of the question marks below with one of the five letters V, W, Y, F or H and then rearrange the letters to form a common word. Each of the five letters will be used only once.

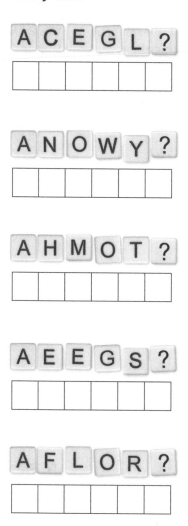

A C E G L ?

A N O W Y ?

A H M O T ?

A E E G S ?

A F L O R ?

BANANA TREES

LEVEL

Use the 18 tiles in this bunch to fill in each of the three grids below. To get you started, a few tiles from the bunch have been placed in each grid, and the BANANA BITES provide hints. Using the remaining tiles in the bunch, find words that complete each grid.

1. **BANANA BITE:** One word is a type of fabric.

2. **BANANA BITE:** One word means "renown."

3. **BANANA BITE:** One word means "weakened."

Tiles: G M I A N E G / A R H W G N G / F M B I

Grid 1 contains: E, H

Grid 2 contains: H, A, G, I

Grid 3 contains: G, A, E, N, I

146

Use the 18 tiles in this bunch to fill in each of the three grids below. To get you started, a few tiles from the bunch have been placed in each grid, and the BANANA BITES provide hints. Using the remaining tiles in the bunch, find words that complete each grid.

1. **BANANA BITE:**
One word means "to raise."

2. **BANANA BITE:**
One word is a type of breakfast food.

3. **BANANA BITE:**
One word is a type of meat.

BANANA PEELS

LEVEL

There is <u>one letter</u> that when added to all of the six-letter words below can be used to form new seven-letter words. Find the letter that works for all four words, add it to each word, and then rearrange each set of letters to form a new word. For example, L can be added to ROADS, WEARY, EPICS and GONER to form DORSAL, LAWYER, SPLICE and LONGER.

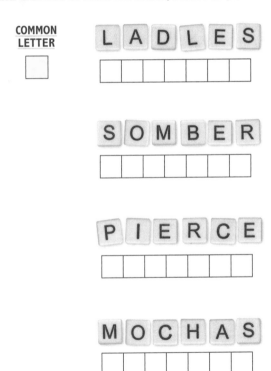

COMMON
LETTER

L A D L E S

S O M B E R

P I E R C E

M O C H A S

For each of the words below, replace one letter with the tile after the plus sign. Then rearrange the letters to spell a word related to chemistry.

U N S P O I L T + O

NUCLEOLE + M

S N O R T I N G + E

R E T A K E + B

A R C H I N G + O

B R A N C H + O

R O U T I N E + N

BANANA FILLING

LEVEL

Add an R **to each of the words below and then rearrange the letters in each word to form a new seven-letter word.**

C I C A D A

⬚ ⬚ ⬚ ⬚ ⬚ ⬚ ⬚

A N A L O G

⬚ ⬚ ⬚ ⬚ ⬚ ⬚ ⬚

L A C I L Y

⬚ ⬚ ⬚ ⬚ ⬚ ⬚ ⬚

M A I M E D

⬚ ⬚ ⬚ ⬚ ⬚ ⬚ ⬚

Using any letters EXCEPT the ones that appear in the bunch below, fill in the blanks to form three new words.

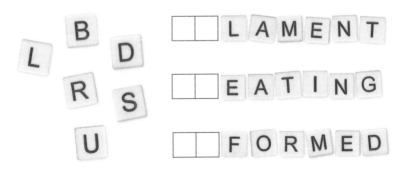

B
L
D
R
S
U

⬚ ⬚ L A M E N T

⬚ ⬚ E A T I N G

⬚ ⬚ F O R M E D

Using five of the tiles from each bunch on the left, fill in the blanks on the right to make an eight-letter word that connects the grid.

BUNCH OF BANANAS

LEVEL

For each phrase below, rearrange the letters to spell two new words that are both female first names. For example, CUTE SNAIL PARTY becomes PETUNIA and CRYSTAL.

GREY FILET ICING

☐☐☐☐☐☐☐☐☐ ☐☐☐☐☐☐

NO I CAN BE GENIAL

☐☐☐☐☐☐☐ ☐☐☐☐☐☐☐☐

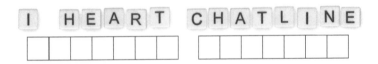

I HEART CHATLINE

☐☐☐☐☐☐☐☐ ☐☐☐☐☐☐☐

A CHROME BATTLER

☐☐☐☐☐☐☐☐☐ ☐☐☐☐☐☐

FEEL CORN ALLURE

☐☐☐☐☐☐☐ ☐☐☐☐☐☐☐☐

Each set of letters below is arranged alphabetically, and the ? is in the correct alphabetical position. Figure out what letter the ? represents and rearrange the letters to spell a six-letter word. For example, in DL?PRUY the ? could be an L, M, N, O or P. Here it represents an O, which can be combined with the other letters to spell PROUDLY.

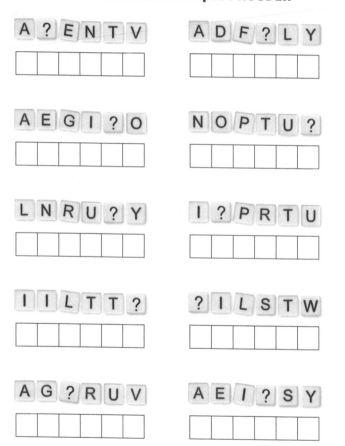

A ? E N T V

A D F ? L Y

A E G I ? O

N O P T U ?

L N R U ? Y

I ? P R T U

I I L T T ?

? I L S T W

A G ? R U V

A E I ? S Y

GO BANANAS!

LEVEL

Use all 21 tiles in this bunch to create a collection of exactly four connecting and intersecting common words in the grid below. **All four of the words must begin with the same letter.** The words may be horizontal or vertical, reading left to right or top to bottom.

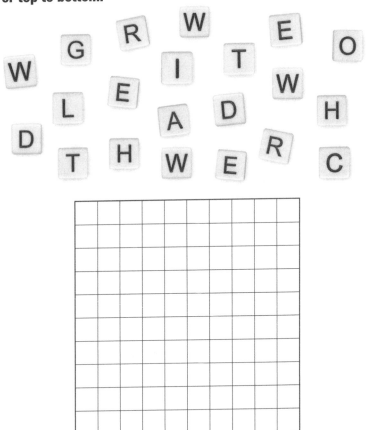

Use all 21 tiles in this bunch to create a collection of exactly four connecting and intersecting common words in the grid below. <u>All four of the words must begin with the same letter.</u> The words may be horizontal or vertical, reading left to right or top to bottom.

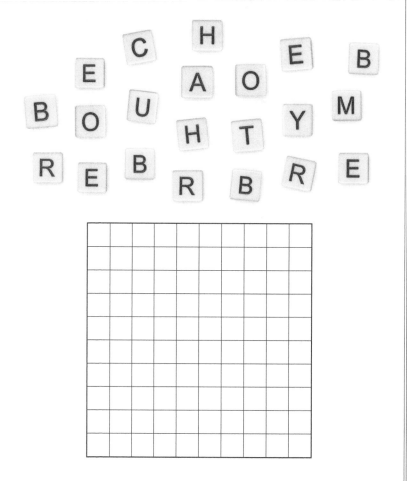

For both of the word groups below, change one letter in the top word to one of the letters that appears in the bottom word, then rearrange the tiles to form a new common word. Do the same with each new word until you arrive at the bottom word. For example, the path from BARK to PLUM is BARK, MARK, RAMP, RUMP, PLUM.

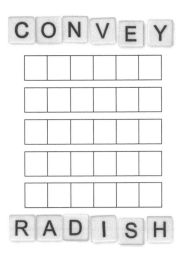

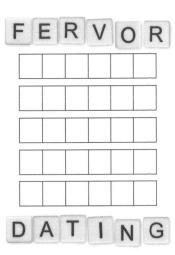

Each of the four-letter words below may be extended both on the right and the left to form an eight-letter word. Drawing from the tiles directly above each word, fill in the blanks to find the longer words as quickly as you can.

A A G I L M U

☐ ☐ B R O S ☐ ☐

A C I L N O T

☐ ☐ A R C H ☐ ☐

A B C E E I P

☐ ☐ S E N T ☐ ☐

A E I N O P R

☐ ☐ N U M B ☐ ☐

A E N O R S S

☐ ☐ B E S T ☐ ☐

For each bunch below, rearrange the letters to form two intersecting words that fit into the corresponding grid.

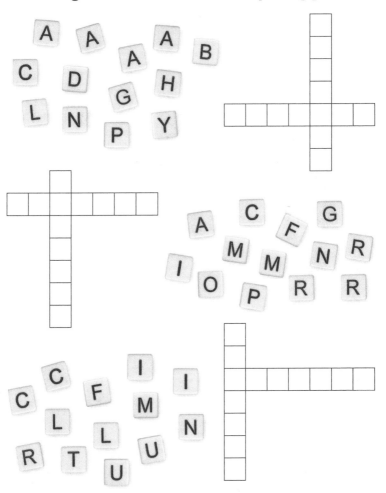

For each of the six words below, add one letter from the word NUCLEI (each letter will be used only once) and then rearrange the letters to spell a country. Once you've filled in all the blanks, take the shaded letters from each line and rearrange them to spell a bonus country.

NUCLEI

SANDLOT

COMIX

DANGLE

REGAIN

BONUS
WORD

SALARIAT

ABUSER

159

BANANA SPLITS

LEVEL

For each of the three words below, change one letter to an I and then rearrange the letters to spell a type of building.

S H O P T A L K

M U S T A R D

F E R R Y M E N

For each of the three words below, change one letter to a C and then rearrange the letters to spell a type of mood or emotion.

D I C T A T E S

S H E I K D O M

U N I V E R S E

Replace each of the question marks below with one of the five letters V , W , Y , F or H and then rearrange the letters to form a common word. Each of the five letters will be used only once.

A D E E E S ?

☐ ☐ ☐ ☐ ☐ ☐ ☐

A C I L P T ?

☐ ☐ ☐ ☐ ☐ ☐ ☐

A A C E M N ?

☐ ☐ ☐ ☐ ☐ ☐ ☐

A D E O T U ?

☐ ☐ ☐ ☐ ☐ ☐ ☐

A C E I M P ?

☐ ☐ ☐ ☐ ☐ ☐ ☐

LEVEL

Use the 18 tiles in this bunch to fill in each of the three grids below. To get you started, a few tiles from the bunch have been placed in each grid. Using the remaining tiles in the bunch, find words that complete each grid.

Use the 18 tiles in this bunch to fill in each of the three grids below. To get you started, a few tiles from the bunch have been placed in each grid. Using the remaining tiles in the bunch, find words that complete each grid.

A E T F H T T
N U O P U R I G
P P U N

1.

E U

G

F O

2.

T U

N

U

3.

I

A

U

U

There is <u>one letter</u> that when added to all of the six-letter words below can be used to form new seven-letter words. Find the letter that works for all four words, add it to each word, and then rearrange each set of letters to form a new word. For example, L can be added to ROADS, WEARY, EPICS and GONER to form DORSAL, LAWYER, SPLICE and LONGER.

COMMON
LETTER

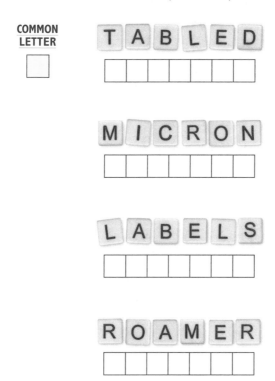

T A B L E D

M I C R O N

L A B E L S

R O A M E R

For each of the words below, replace one letter with the tile after the plus sign. Then rearrange the letters to spell one word from the name of a Beatles song.

S H L E M I E L + C

S A I N T D O M + D

W A N D E R I N G + O

C R A B A P P L E + K

S O N G S M I T H + E

N U R S E M A I D + B

S E D E N T A R Y + Y

BANANA FILLING

LEVEL

Add a C **to each of the words below and then rearrange the letters in each word to form a new eight-letter word.**

H O A R D E R

☐ ☐ ☐ ☐ ☐ ☐ ☐ ☐

G A L L E O N

☐ ☐ ☐ ☐ ☐ ☐ ☐ ☐

R E A D M I T

☐ ☐ ☐ ☐ ☐ ☐ ☐ ☐

Using any letters EXCEPT the ones that appear in the bunch below, fill in the blanks to form three new words.

☐ ☐ E A T A B L E

☐ ☐ C L O S U R E

☐ ☐ I N L A N D S

Using five of the tiles from each bunch on the left, fill in the blanks on the right to make an eight-letter word that connects the grid.

BUNCH OF BANANAS

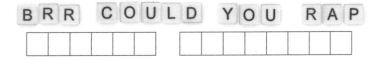

LEVEL

For each word or phrase below, rearrange the letters to spell two new words that are both kinds of fabric. For example, **A CONCRETE PLOT** becomes **COTTON** and **PERCALE**.

LOATHING A COLOR

BRR COULD YOU RAP

FELLING HANGMAN

CHASE TRAIL HOME

Each set of letters below is arranged alphabetically, and the ? is in the correct alphabetical position. Figure out what letter the ? represents and rearrange the letters to spell a seven-letter word. For example, in DL?PRUY the ? could be an L, M, N, O or P. Here it represents an O, which can be combined with the other letters to spell PROUDLY.

A A B C E ? N

A A E N R R ?

A A I N N R ?

A B E G M ? U

C D E F I ? T

C D E ? L O W

A B E ? L U Y

C E E G L ? T

C E F F I S ?

E E M N ? T U

Use all 21 tiles in this bunch to create a collection of connecting and intersecting common words in the grid below. Any word that has more than two letters must be a color. The words may be horizontal or vertical, reading left to right or top to bottom.

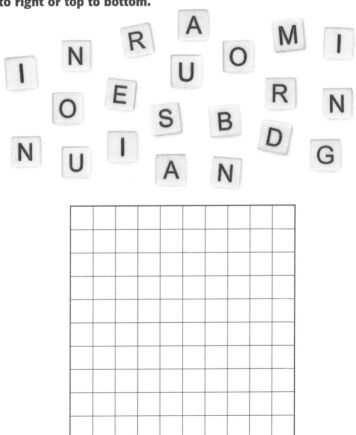

Use all 21 tiles in this bunch to create a collection of connecting and intersecting common words in the grid below. <u>Any word that has more than two letters must be a type of animal.</u> The words may be horizontal or vertical, reading left to right or top to bottom.

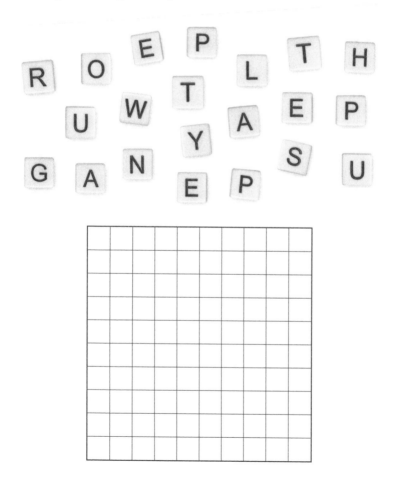

LEVEL

For both of the word groups below, change one letter in the top word to one of the letters that appears in the bottom word, then rearrange the tiles to form a new common word. Do the same with each new word until you arrive at the bottom word. For example, a path from BARK to PLUM is BARK, MARK, RAMP, RUMP, PLUM.

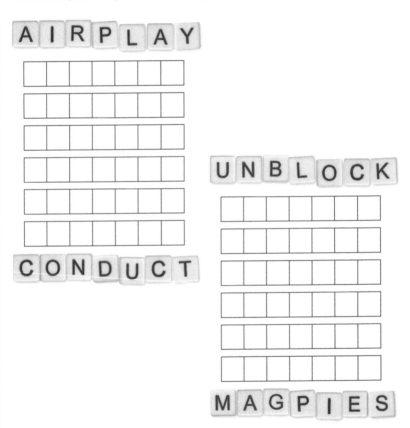

Each of the three-letter words below may be extended both on the right and the left to form a nine-letter word. Drawing from the tiles directly above each word, fill in the blanks to find the longer words as quickly as you can.

TOP BANANA

LEVEL

For each bunch below, rearrange the letters to form two intersecting words that fit into the corresponding grid.

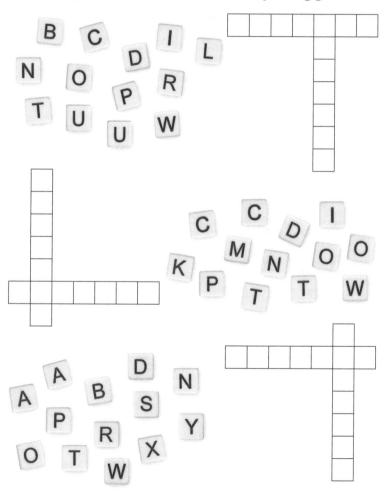

For each of the six words below, add one letter from the word FATTEN (each letter will be used only once) and then rearrange the letters to spell a color. Once you've filled in all the blanks, take the shaded letters from each line and rearrange them to spell a bonus color.

F A T T E N

C H I A U S

N U C L E A R

M U D R A S

G R A T I N E E

M A N A G E

M E L D E R

BONUS WORD

BANANA SPLITS

LEVEL

For each of the three words below, change one letter to an A **and then rearrange the letters to spell a condition or disease.**

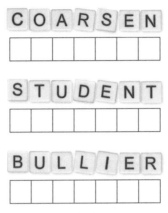

C O A R S E N

☐ ☐ ☐ ☐ ☐ ☐ ☐

S T U D E N T

☐ ☐ ☐ ☐ ☐ ☐ ☐

B U L L I E R

☐ ☐ ☐ ☐ ☐ ☐ ☐

For each of the three words below, change one letter to an A **and then rearrange the letters to spell a word that contains the name of a mammal. For example, TREBLED would become BER<u>AT</u>ED.**

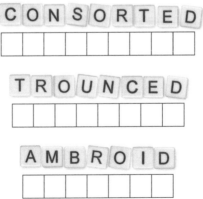

C O N S O R T E D

☐ ☐ ☐ ☐ ☐ ☐ ☐ ☐ ☐

T R O U N C E D

☐ ☐ ☐ ☐ ☐ ☐ ☐ ☐

A M B R O I D

☐ ☐ ☐ ☐ ☐ ☐ ☐

Replace each of the question marks below with one of the five letters V, W, Y, F or H and then rearrange the letters to form a common word. Each of the five letters will be used only once.

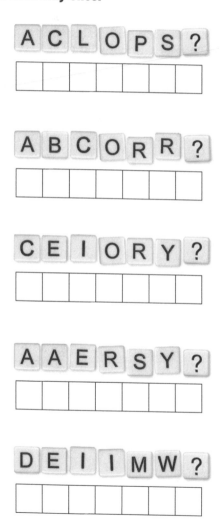

A C L O P S ?

A B C O R R ?

C E I O R Y ?

A A E R S Y ?

D E I I M W ?

LEVEL

Use the 18 tiles in this bunch to fill in each of the three grids below. To get you started, a few tiles from the bunch have been placed in each grid. Using the remaining tiles in the bunch, find words that complete each grid.

Use the 18 tiles in this bunch to fill in each of the three grids below. To get you started, a few tiles from the bunch have been placed in each grid. Using the remaining tiles in the bunch, find words that complete each grid.

BANANA PEELS

LEVEL

There is <u>one letter</u> that when added to all of the six-letter words below can be used to form new seven-letter words. Find the letter that works for all four words, add it to each word, and then rearrange each set of letters to form a new word. For example, L can be added to ROADS, WEARY, EPICS and GONER to form DORSAL, LAWYER, SPLICE and LONGER.

COMMON
LETTER

A R C A D E

R A N C O R

A D M I R E

C H E S T S

180

For each of the words below, replace one letter with the tile after the plus sign. Then rearrange the letters to spell the last name of a Baseball Hall of Famer.

E L E M E N T S + C

R E S A D D L E + Y

H A R D C O R E + U

C H A I R M A N + L

W A S H W O M E N + T

S A L A M I + U

L A T E R A L S + G

BANANA FILLING

LEVEL

Add a **B** to each of the words below and then rearrange the letters in each word to form a new eight-letter word.

S O L A T I A

☐☐☐☐☐☐☐☐

C L E A R E R

☐☐☐☐☐☐☐☐

R E D R I V E

☐☐☐☐☐☐☐☐

Using any letters EXCEPT the ones that appear in the bunch below, fill in the blanks to form three new words.

C
L R
T

☐☐ C O A S T A L

☐☐ D E C A G O N

☐☐ V I O L A T E

Using five of the tiles from each bunch on the left, fill in the blanks on the right to make an eight-letter word that connects the grid.

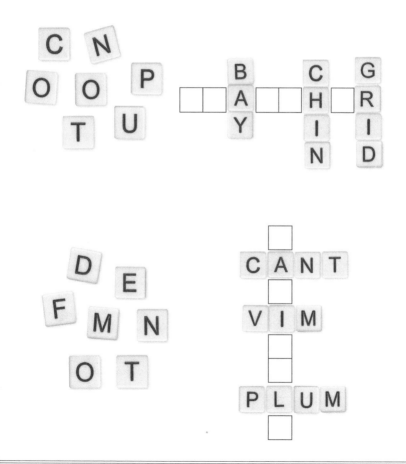

BUNCH OF BANANAS

LEVEL

For each word or phrase below, rearrange the letters to spell two new words that are either something you read or something you write. For example, **HIP BOROUGH ARMY** becomes **HUMOR** and **BIOGRAPHY**.

CYANIDE ARMOR

ROUGH COBBLER

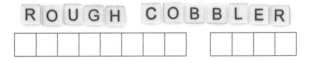

YAWNER STOPPERS

NOT A PRIZE GAMER

Each set of letters below is arranged alphabetically, and the ? **is in the correct alphabetical position. Figure out what letter the** ? **represents and rearrange the letters to spell a seven-letter word. For example, in DL?PRUY the ? could be an L, M, N, O or P. Here it represents an O, which can be combined with the other letters to spell PROUDLY.**

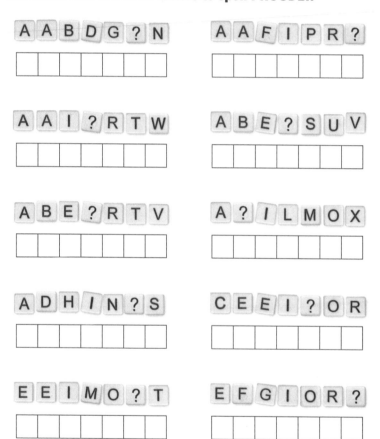

A A B D G ? N

A A F I P R ?

A A I ? R T W

A B E ? S U V

A B E ? R T V

A ? I L M O X

A D H I N ? S

C E E I ? O R

E E I M O ? T

E F G I O R ?

GO BANANAS! LEVEL

Use all 21 tiles in this bunch to create a collection of connecting and intersecting common words in the grid below. **Any word that has more than two letters must be the name of a nation.** The words may be horizontal or vertical, reading left to right or top to bottom.

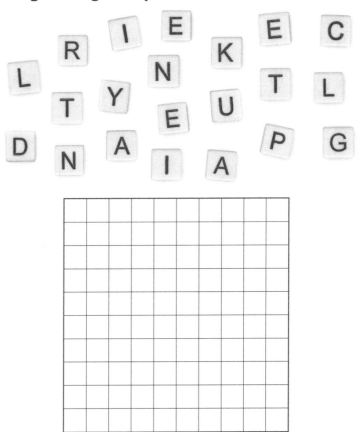

Use all 21 tiles in this bunch to create a collection of connecting and intersecting common words in the grid below. **Any word that has more than two letters must be the last name of an Oscar-winning actress.** The words may be horizontal or vertical, reading left to right or top to bottom.

For both of the word groups below, change one letter in the top word to one of the letters that appears in the bottom word, then rearrange the tiles to form a new common word. Do the same with each new word until you arrive at the bottom word. For example, a path from BARK to PLUM is BARK, MARK, RAMP, RUMP, PLUM.

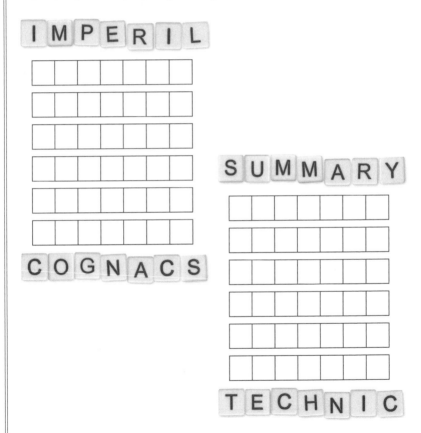

IMPERIL

COGNACS

SUMMARY

TECHNIC

Each of the three-letter words below may be extended both on the right and the left to form a nine-letter word. Drawing from the tiles directly above each word, fill in the blanks to find the longer words as quickly as you can.

A A B C H M R

⬚ ⬚ ⬚ **L E G** ⬚ ⬚ ⬚

A A C E N R T

⬚ ⬚ ⬚ **D I D** ⬚ ⬚ ⬚

A D E M P R S

⬚ ⬚ ⬚ **S A C** ⬚ ⬚ ⬚

A I L M N O P

⬚ ⬚ ⬚ **I C E** ⬚ ⬚ ⬚

C I M N O U Y

⬚ ⬚ ⬚ **T A G** ⬚ ⬚ ⬚

189

TOP BANANA

LEVEL

For each bunch below, rearrange the letters to form two intersecting words that fit into the corresponding grid.

For each of the six words below, add one letter from the word **THORNS** (each letter will be used only once) and then rearrange the letters to spell a word that describes a group of people. Once you've filled in all the blanks, take the shaded letters from each line and rearrange them to spell a bonus group.

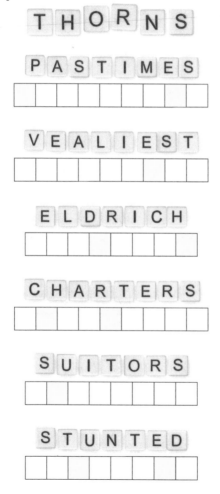

T H O R N S

P A S T I M E S

V E A L I E S T

E L D R I C H

BONUS WORD

C H A R T E R S

S U I T O R S

S T U N T E D

For each of the three words below, change one letter to a T **and then rearrange the letters to spell a condition or disease.**

O V E R B I G

[ ][ ][ ][ ][ ][ ][ ]

R E S O A K

[ ][ ][ ][ ][ ][ ]

S L I C K E R

[ ][ ][ ][ ][ ][ ][ ]

For each of the three words below, change one letter to a V **and then rearrange the letters to spell the last name of a famous author.**

C A B E R N E T S

[ ][ ][ ][ ][ ][ ][ ][ ][ ]

N O N G U E S T

[ ][ ][ ][ ][ ][ ][ ][ ][ ]

B O O K M A N

[ ][ ][ ][ ][ ][ ][ ]

192

Replace each of the question marks below with one of the five letters V, W, Y, F or H and then rearrange the letters to form a common word. Each of the five letters will be used only once.

A C I P R Y ?

B E I N O R ?

E E I N N T ?

A G H N T U ?

A C D O R R ?

Use the 18 tiles in this bunch to fill in each of the three grids below. To get you started, a few tiles from the bunch have been placed in each grid. Using the remaining tiles in the bunch, find words that complete each grid.

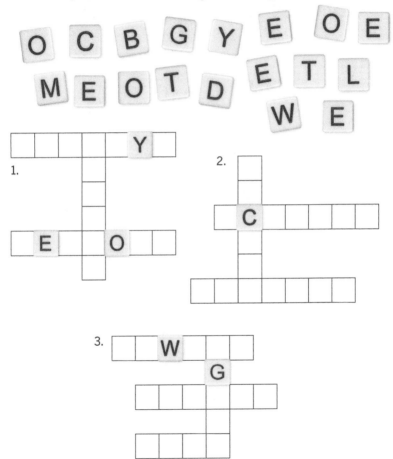

Use the 18 tiles in this bunch to fill in each of the three grids below. To get you started, a few tiles from the bunch have been placed in each grid. Using the remaining tiles in the bunch, find words that complete each grid.

BANANA PEELS

LEVEL

There is <u>one letter</u> that when added to all of the six-letter words below can be used to form new seven-letter words. Find the letter that works for all four words, add it to each word, and then rearrange each set of letters to form a new word. For example, L can be added to ROADS, WEARY, EPICS and GONER to form DORSAL, LAWYER, SPLICE and LONGER.

COMMON
LETTER

C A P O N S

☐☐☐☐☐☐☐

H A I R E D

☐☐☐☐☐☐☐

L E A N E R

☐☐☐☐☐☐☐

P I R A T E

☐☐☐☐☐☐☐

For each of the words below, replace one letter with the tile after the plus sign. Then rearrange the letters to spell one word from the name of a film that won an Oscar for Best Picture.

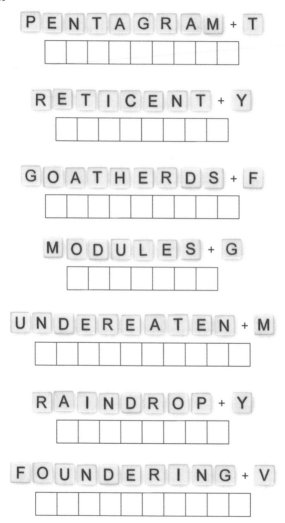

P E N T A G R A M + T

R E T I C E N T + Y

G O A T H E R D S + F

M O D U L E S + G

U N D E R E A T E N + M

R A I N D R O P + Y

F O U N D E R I N G + V

BANANA FILLING

LEVEL

Add a `T` **to each of the words below and then rearrange the letters in each word to form a new eight-letter word.**

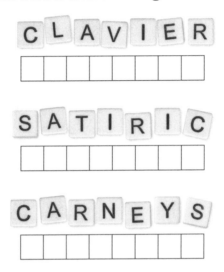

C L A V I E R

S A T I R I C

C A R N E Y S

Using any letters EXCEPT the ones that appear in the bunch below, fill in the blanks to form three new words.

U D E L C P

☐ ☐ C I T A B L E

☐ ☐ E N C H A N T

☐ ☐ E A S I E S T

Using five of the tiles from each bunch on the left, fill in
the blanks on the right to make an eight-letter word that
connects the grid.

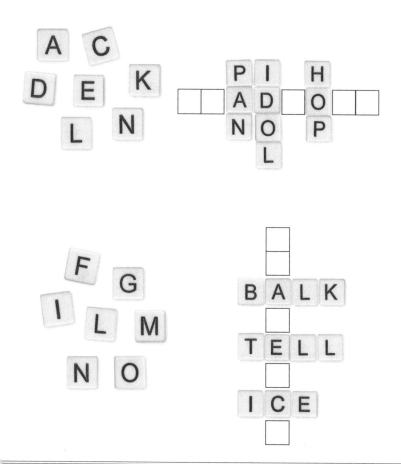

BUNCH OF BANANAS

LEVEL

For each word or phrase below, rearrange the letters to spell the title of a famous novel. For example, **SAFE ORDER THANKS** becomes **HEART OF DARKNESS**.

HE FORGETS WARPATH

CAT TOOT A WISE LIFE

CROP HELP TO RULE

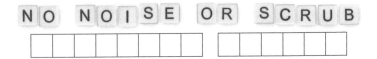

NO NOISE OR SCRUB

Each set of letters below is arranged alphabetically, and the ? is in the correct alphabetical position. Figure out what letter the ? represents and then rearrange the letters to spell a seven-letter word. For example, in DL?PRUY the ? could be an L, M, N, O or P. Here it represents an O, which can be combined with the other letters to spell PROUDLY.

A A B G I ? R

A A H R S ? Y

A B C E E N ?

A A E L ? T U

A C E E N ? Y

A C E O P T ?

C D I O P R ?

C E E L T T ?

E E L R R V ?

E F I N N O ?

GO BANANAS!

LEVEL

Use all 21 tiles in this bunch to create a collection of connecting and intersecting common words in the grid below. Any word that has more than two letters must be a name from one of the Star Wars movies. The words may be horizontal or vertical, reading left to right or top to bottom.

Use all 21 tiles in this bunch to create a collection of connecting and intersecting common words in the grid below. <u>Any word that has more than two letters must be the last name of a fictional movie hero.</u> The words may be horizontal or vertical, reading left to right or top to bottom.

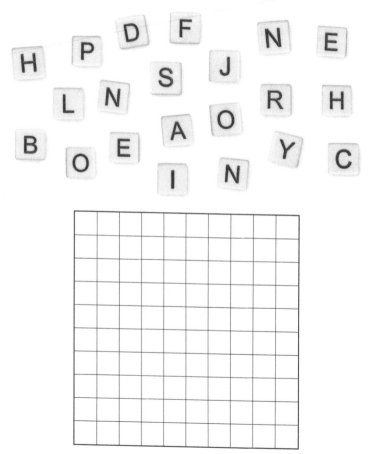

LEVEL

For both of the word groups below, change one letter in the top word to one of the letters that appears in the bottom word, then rearrange the tiles to form a new common word. Do the same with each new word until you arrive at the bottom word. For example, the path from BARK to PLUM is BARK, MARK, RAMP, RUMP, PLUM.

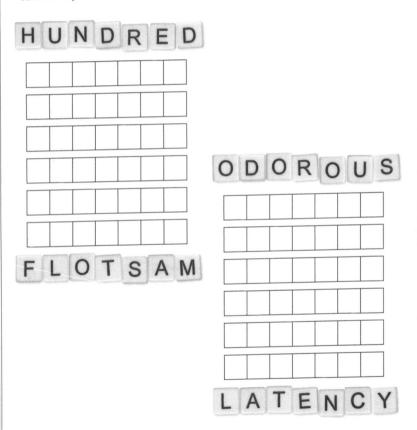

HUNDRED

FLOTSAM

ODOROUS

LATENCY

Each of the three-letter words below may be extended both on the right and the left to form a nine-letter word. Drawing from the tiles directly above each word, fill in the blanks to find the longer words as quickly as you can.

A D E I N S T
[ ][ ][ ] T E W [ ][ ][ ]

A A B C G L R
[ ][ ][ ] P E T [ ][ ][ ]

A C E K L R R
[ ][ ][ ] E T A [ ][ ][ ]

A E N O S T Y
[ ][ ][ ] C O P [ ][ ][ ]

D E F I L M S
[ ][ ][ ] E A T [ ][ ][ ]

TOP BANANA

LEVEL

For each bunch below, rearrange the letters to form two intersecting words that fit into the corresponding grid.

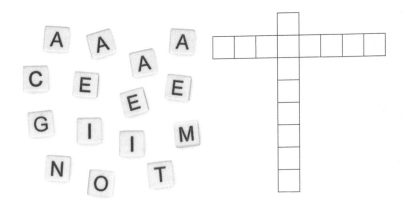

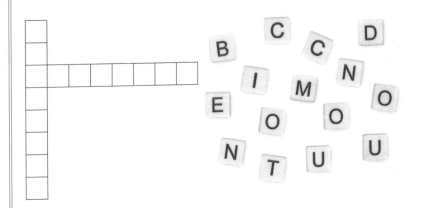

For each of the six words below, add one letter from the word AVOWAL (each letter will be used only once) and then rearrange the letters to spell a kind of animal. Once you've filled in all the blanks, take the shaded letters from each line and rearrange them to spell a bonus animal.

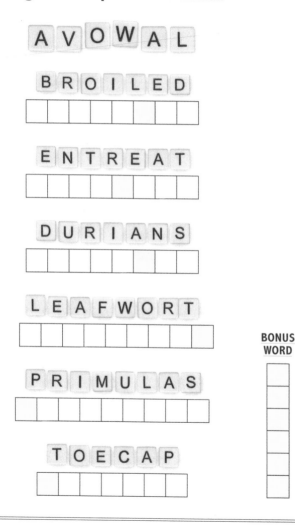

A V O W A L

BROILED

ENTREAT

DURIANS

LEAFWORT

PRIMULAS

TOECAP

BONUS WORD

For each of the three words below, change one letter to an E **and then rearrange the letters to spell a word of Spanish origin.**

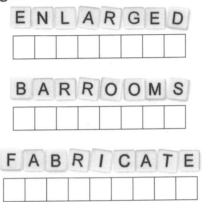

E N L A R G E D

B A R R O O M S

F A B R I C A T E

For each of the three words below, change one letter to a U **and then rearrange the letters to spell a type of building.**

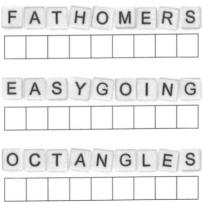

F A T H O M E R S

E A S Y G O I N G

O C T A N G L E S

208

Replace each of the question marks below with one of the five letters V, W, Y, F or H and then rearrange the letters to form a common word. Each of the five letters will be used only once.

A A B L L S T ?

A E I I L N R ?

A G I I L N T ?

A E G I K L N ?

A E G R S T T ?

BANANA TREES

LEVEL

Use the 22 tiles in this bunch to fill in the two grids below. To get you started, a few tiles from the bunch have been placed in each grid. Using the remaining tiles in the bunch, find words that complete each grid.

1.

		W		O		
	D					
	T					

2.

			P		N	
		P			D	

Use the 22 tiles in this bunch to fill in the two grids below. To get you started, a few tiles from the bunch have been placed in each grid. Using the remaining tiles in the bunch, find words that complete each grid.

1.

2.

BANANA PEELS

LEVEL

There is <u>one letter</u> that when added to all of the seven-letter words below can be used to form new eight-letter words. Find the letter that works for all four words, add it to each word, and then rearrange each set of letters to form a new word. For example, L can be added to ROADS, WEARY, EPICS and GONER to form DORSAL, LAWYER, SPLICE and LONGER.

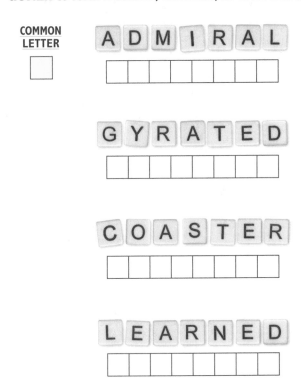

COMMON
LETTER

ADMIRAL

GYRATED

COASTER

LEARNED

For each of the words below, replace one letter with the tile after the plus sign. Then rearrange the letters to spell a type of invention.

V E L O C I T I E S + N

D R E A M B O A T S + K

R E P A C K A G E + M

O U T S E L L I N G + I

S P I R O C H E T E + L

M E T A P H O R S + U

O V E R S L E P T + Y

BANANA FILLING

LEVEL

Add a D **to each of the words below and then rearrange the letters in each word to form a new nine-letter word.**

T R A C H E A L

[ ][ ][ ][ ][ ][ ][ ][ ][ ]

S P E A R M A N

[ ][ ][ ][ ][ ][ ][ ][ ][ ]

S C A L E P A N

[ ][ ][ ][ ][ ][ ][ ][ ][ ]

Using any letters EXCEPT the ones that appear in the bunch below, fill in the blanks to form three new words.

[ ][ ] O P E R A T E D

R   T

U

[ ][ ] B A S E M E N T

[ ][ ] S O L V A B L E

Using six of the tiles from each bunch on the left, fill in the blanks on the right to make a nine-letter word that connects the grid.

BUNCH OF BANANAS

LEVEL

For each phrase below, rearrange the letters to spell two words that mean the opposite of each other. For example, LETS SLICE INTEGERS becomes ENERGETIC and LISTLESS.

WAVE URBAN SENATOR

☐☐☐☐☐☐☐☐☐ ☐☐☐☐☐☐☐

FORGES A SUNDAE

☐☐☐☐☐☐☐☐ ☐☐☐☐☐

DATA CURE MAN MIND

☐☐☐☐☐☐☐ ☐☐☐☐☐☐☐☐

LAMP STOMPED ICICLE

☐☐☐☐☐☐☐☐☐☐ ☐☐☐☐☐☐☐

I FAULT BLUE GUY

☐☐☐☐☐☐☐☐☐ ☐☐☐☐☐

Each set of letters below is arranged alphabetically, and the [?] is in the correct alphabetical position. Figure out what letter the [?] represents and rearrange the letters to spell an eight-letter word. For example, in DL?PRUY the ? could be an L, M, N, O or P. Here it represents an O, which can be combined with the other letters to spell PROUDLY.

C ? I R S T U Y

C H O ? S T T U

C ? L N O R S U

B ? G L L O R U

B E ? O O R R S

B E I L O P P ?

E H K M O O R ?

A I I L N O P ?

A ? O P S T U W

A ? H I L P S W

GO BANANAS!

LEVEL

Use all 21 tiles in this bunch to create a collection of connecting and intersecting common words in the grid below. <u>Each word must contain at least six letters.</u> The words may be horizontal or vertical, reading left to right or top to bottom.

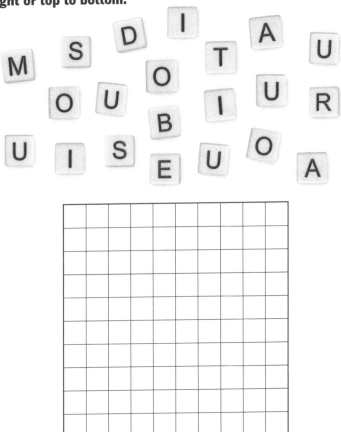

Use all 21 tiles in this bunch to create a collection of connecting and intersecting common words in the grid below. **Each word must contain at least six letters.** The words may be horizontal or vertical, reading left to right or top to bottom.

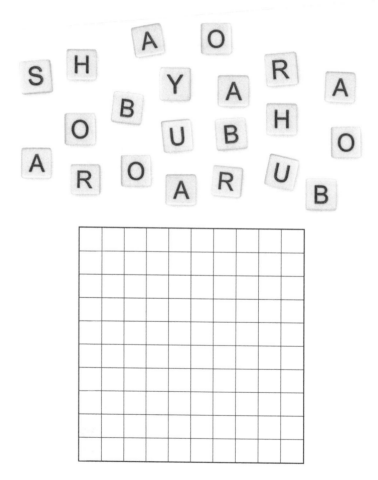

For the word group below, change one letter in the top word to one of the letters that appears in the bottom word, then rearrange the tiles to form a new common word. Do the same with each new word until you arrive at the bottom word. For example, a path from BARK to PLUM is BARK, MARK, RAMP, RUMP, PLUM.

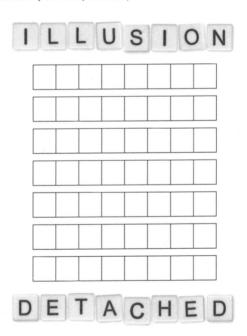

I L L U S I O N

D E T A C H E D

Each of the four-letter words below may be extended both on the right and the left to form a ten-letter word. Drawing from the tiles directly above each word, fill in the blanks to find the longer words as quickly as you can.

A A D E F I O

☐ ☐ ☐ C I O N ☐ ☐ ☐

A B C I L N S

☐ ☐ ☐ L I S T ☐ ☐ ☐

C E E H N R T

☐ ☐ ☐ T I M E ☐ ☐ ☐

E G I L N T Y

☐ ☐ ☐ E R O S ☐ ☐ ☐

A H I I M P S

☐ ☐ ☐ O V E R ☐ ☐ ☐

For each bunch below, rearrange the letters to form two intersecting words that fit into the corresponding grid.

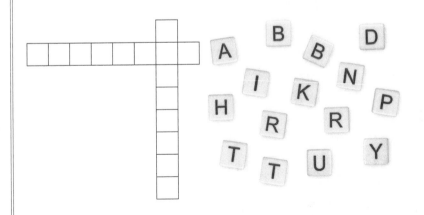

For each of the six words below, add one letter from the word BITTEN (each letter will be used only once) and then rearrange the letters to spell a word related to computers. Once you've filled in all the blanks, take the shaded letters from each line and rearrange them to spell a bonus computer word.

B I T T E N

K N O W E R

□ □ □ □ □ □ □

M I D T O W N

□ □ □ □ □ □ □ □

S U B S U M E

□ □ □ □ □ □ □

T O Y L I K E

□ □ □ □ □ □ □

C E N T A U R

□ □ □ □ □ □ □

C U R T S E Y

□ □ □ □ □ □ □

BONUS
WORD

□
□
□
□
□
□
□
□

223

For each of the three words below, change one letter to an N **and then rearrange the letters to spell a condition or disease.**

M E D I C A T E

E N G A G E R S

T U I T I O N S

For each of the three words below, change one letter to an L **and then rearrange the letters to spell a one-word movie title.**

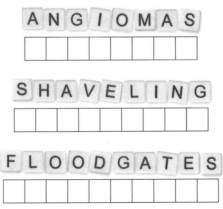

A N G I O M A S

S H A V E L I N G

F L O O D G A T E S

Replace each of the question marks below with one of the five letters V, W, Y, F or H and then rearrange the letters to form a common word. Each of the five letters will be used only once.

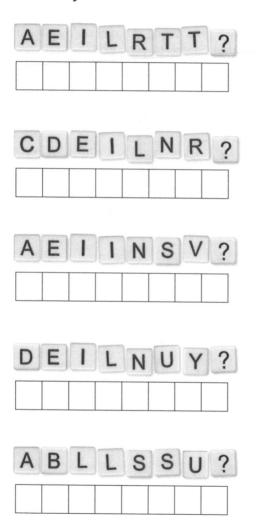

A E I L R T T ?

C D E I L N R ?

A E I I N S V ?

D E I L N U Y ?

A B L L S S U ?

Use the 22 tiles in this bunch to fill in the two grids below. To get you started, a few tiles from the bunch have been placed in each grid. Using the remaining tiles in the bunch, find words that complete each grid.

1.

2.

Use the 22 tiles in this bunch to fill in the two grids below. To get you started, a few tiles from the bunch have been placed in each grid. Using the remaining tiles in the bunch, find words that complete each grid.

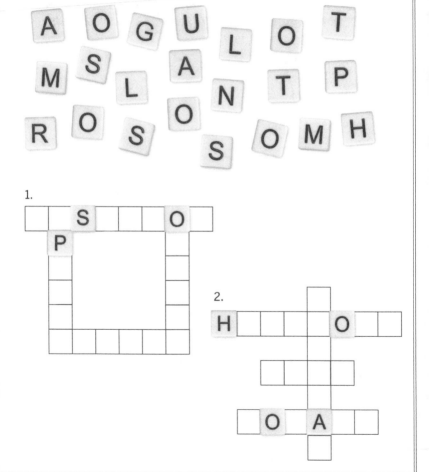

1.

2.

There is <u>one letter</u> that when added to all of the seven-letter words below can be used to form new eight-letter words. Find the letter that works for all four words, add it to each word, and then rearrange each set of letters to form a new word. For example, L can be added to ROADS, WEARY, EPICS and GONER to form DORSAL, LAWYER, SPLICE and LONGER.

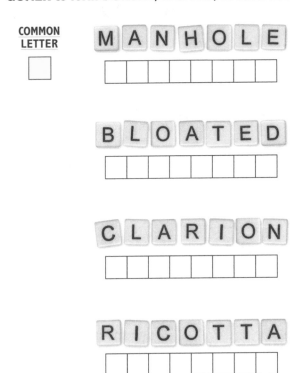

COMMON LETTER

MANHOLE

BLOATED

CLARION

RICOTTA

228

For each of the words below, replace one letter with the tile after the plus sign. Then rearrange the letters to spell a type of bug.

E R R A T I C A L L Y + P

[ ][ ][ ][ ][ ][ ][ ][ ][ ][ ][ ]

A M Y G D U L E + B

[ ][ ][ ][ ][ ][ ][ ][ ]

R I F L E R Y + F

[ ][ ][ ][ ][ ][ ][ ]

A D O R I N G L Y + F

[ ][ ][ ][ ][ ][ ][ ][ ][ ]

D E C E P T I O N + E

[ ][ ][ ][ ][ ][ ][ ][ ][ ]

P O I S O N E R + C

[ ][ ][ ][ ][ ][ ][ ][ ]

R E F U T A B L Y + T

[ ][ ][ ][ ][ ][ ][ ][ ][ ]

BANANA FILLING

LEVEL

Add a G to each of the words below and then rearrange the letters in each word to form a new nine-letter word.

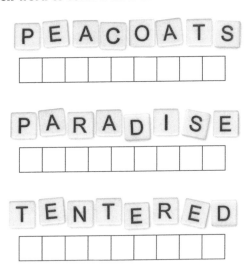

P E A C O A T S

☐ ☐ ☐ ☐ ☐ ☐ ☐ ☐ ☐

P A R A D I S E

☐ ☐ ☐ ☐ ☐ ☐ ☐ ☐ ☐

T E N T E R E D

☐ ☐ ☐ ☐ ☐ ☐ ☐ ☐ ☐

Using any letters EXCEPT the ones that appear in the bunch below, fill in the blanks to form three new words.

☐ ☐ R E A D I E S T

C D

☐ ☐ L A X A T I O N

U

☐ ☐ T R O L L I N G

Using six of the tiles from each bunch on the left, fill in the blanks on the right to make an nine-letter word that connects the grid.

BUNCH OF BANANAS

LEVEL

For each word or phrase below, rearrange the letters to spell two words from famous quotes. (The words aren't necessarily adjacent in the quote.) For example, SEE GRAND QUERY becomes ENERGY and SQUARED. (From Albert Einstein's "Energy equals the mass times the speed of light squared.")

232

Each set of letters below is arranged alphabetically, and the ? is in the correct alphabetical position. Figure out what letter the ? represents and then rearrange the letters to spell an eight-letter word. For example, in DL?PRUY the ? could be an L, M, N, O or P. Here it represents an O, which can be combined with the other letters to spell PROUDLY.

GO BANANAS!

LEVEL

Use all 21 tiles in this bunch to create a collection of connecting and intersecting common words in the grid below. **Each word must contain at least six letters.** The words may be horizontal or vertical, reading left to right or top to bottom.

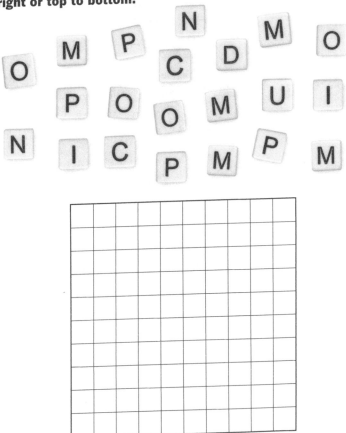

Use all 21 tiles in this bunch to create a collection of connecting and intersecting common words in the grid below. **Each word must contain at least six letters.** The words may be horizontal or vertical, reading left to right or top to bottom.

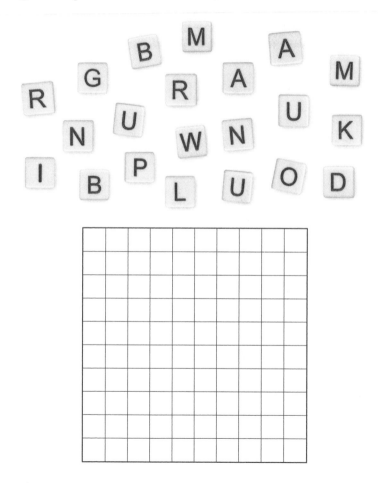

BANANA BOATS

LEVEL

For both of the word groups below, change one letter in the
top word to one of the letters that appears in the bottom
word, then rearrange the tiles to form a new common word.
Do the same with each new word until you arrive at the
bottom word. For example, the path from BARK to PLUM
is BARK, MARK, RAMP, RUMP, PLUM.

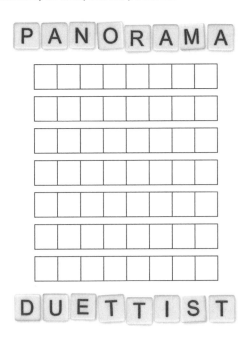

P A N O R A M A

D U E T T I S T

Each of the four-letter words below may be extended both on the right and the left to form a ten-letter word. Drawing from the tiles directly above each word, fill in the blanks to find the longer words as quickly as you can.

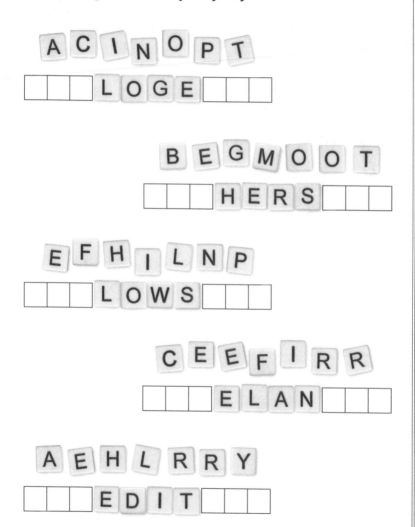

A C I N O P T

☐ ☐ ☐ L O G E ☐ ☐ ☐

B E G M O O T

☐ ☐ ☐ H E R S ☐ ☐ ☐

E F H I L N P

☐ ☐ ☐ L O W S ☐ ☐ ☐

C E E F I R R

☐ ☐ ☐ E L A N ☐ ☐ ☐

A E H L R R Y

☐ ☐ ☐ E D I T ☐ ☐ ☐

237

LEVEL

For each bunch below, rearrange the letters to form two intersecting words that fit into the corresponding grid.

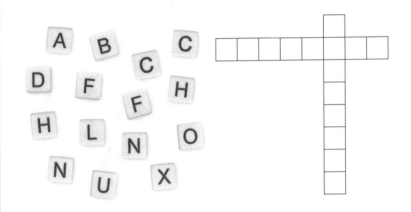

For each of the six words below, add one letter from the word ATOMIC (each letter will be used only once) and then rearrange the letters to spell a word related to the legal profession. Once you've filled in all the blanks, take the shaded letters from each line and rearrange them to spell a bonus legal word.

A T O M I C

S C A L A D E

B A S I N A L

T E R R A N E

T I L T I N G

BONUS
WORD

S I M I L A R

N E A R L Y

BANANA SPLITS

LEVEL

For each of the three words below, change one letter to an A and then rearrange the letters to spell a compound word made from two four-letter words.

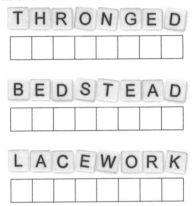

T H R O N G E D

B E D S T E A D

L A C E W O R K

For each of the three words below, change one letter to an O and then rearrange the letters to spell a compound word made from a five-letter and a four-letter word.

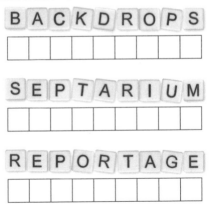

B A C K D R O P S

S E P T A R I U M

R E P O R T A G E

Replace each of the question marks below with one of the five letters V, W, Y, F or H and then rearrange the letters to form a common word. Each of the five letters will be used only once.

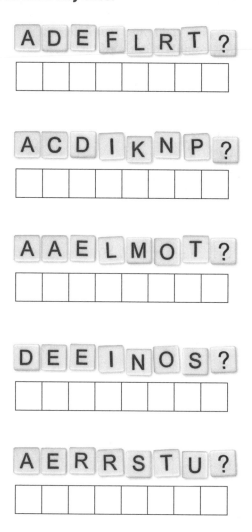

A D E F L R T ?

A C D I K N P ?

A A E L M O T ?

D E E I N O S ?

A E R R S T U ?

BANANA TREES

LEVEL

Use the 22 tiles in this bunch to fill in the two grids below. To get you started, a few tiles from the bunch have been placed in each grid. Using the remaining tiles in the bunch, find words that complete each grid.

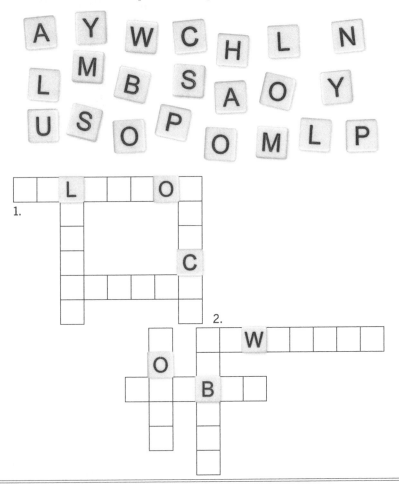

Use the 22 tiles in this bunch to fill in the two grids below. To get you started, a few tiles from the bunch have been placed in each grid. Using the remaining tiles in the bunch, find words that complete each grid.

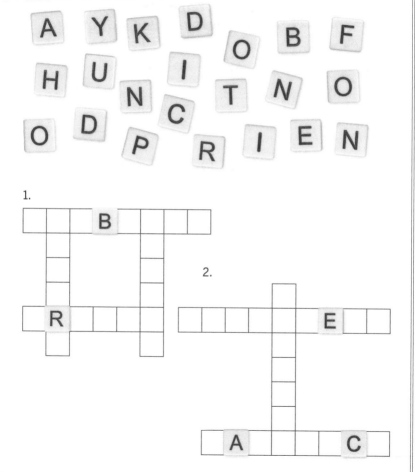

1.

2.

There is <u>one letter</u> that when added to all of the seven-letter words below can be used to form new eight-letter words. Find the letter that works for all four words, add it to each word, and then rearrange each set of letters to form a new word. For example, L can be added to ROADS, WEARY, EPICS and GONER to form DORSAL, LAWYER, SPLICE and LONGER.

COMMON LETTER

C A N A P E S

S A N D A L S

G A S T R E A

A G R O U N D

For each of the words below, replace one letter with the tile after the plus sign. Then rearrange the letters to spell a type of plant.

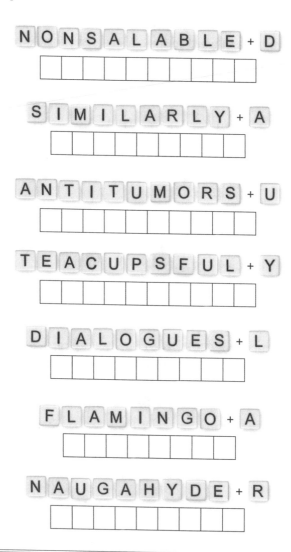

N O N S A L A B L E + D

S I M I L A R L Y + A

A N T I T U M O R S + U

T E A C U P S F U L + Y

D I A L O G U E S + L

F L A M I N G O + A

N A U G A H Y D E + R

BANANA FILLING

LEVEL

Add an M to each of the words below and then rearrange the letters in each word to form a new nine-letter word.

C A T E R A N S

☐☐☐☐☐☐☐☐☐

P A N E T E L A

☐☐☐☐☐☐☐☐☐

C A L L I O P E

☐☐☐☐☐☐☐☐☐

Using any letters EXCEPT the ones that appear in the bunch below, fill in the blanks to form three new words.

☐☐ T R I G G E R S

L N

R

☐☐ G E N E R A T E

☐☐ R A T I F I E D

246

Using six of the tiles from each bunch on the left, fill in the blanks on the right to make a nine-letter word that connects the grid.

For each phrase below, rearrange the letters to spell two words that each contain at least two pairs of the same consonant. (The pairs don't necessarily appear consecutively in the word.) For example, A CURLY TAN NOT REAL becomes RETROACT (with a pair of R's and a pair of T's) and ANNUALLY (with a pair of N's and a pair of L's).

CLASSY SLY MONSOON

PRO BEAT BOP WINNER

CANNOT HIT ATTACHE

CONSIDER CORN SEED

Each set of letters below is arranged alphabetically, and the ? is in the correct alphabetical position. Figure out what letter the ? represents and rearrange the letters to spell an eight-letter word. For example, in DL?PRUY the ? could be an L, M, N, O or P. Here it represents an O, which can be combined with the other letters to spell PROUDLY.

A A ? E L N P Y

A A D E ? L M P

A I I P R R S ?

A B D E H ? R U

A B D I I N O ?

A B E E N O ? S

A B ? N P R T U

A C E E K L ? R

A C G I L ? S U

A C H ? M O R S

GO BANANAS!

LEVEL

Use all 21 tiles in this bunch to create a collection of connecting and intersecting common words in the grid below. **Each word must contain at least six letters.** The words may be horizontal or vertical, reading left to right or top to bottom.

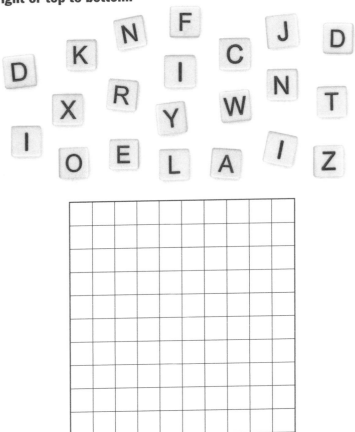

Use all 21 tiles in this bunch to create a collection of connecting and intersecting common words in the grid below. **Each word must contain at least six letters.** The words may be horizontal or vertical, reading left to right or top to bottom.

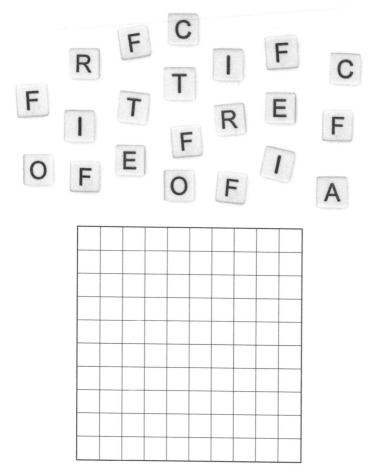

For the word group below, change one letter in the top word to one of the letters that appears in the bottom word, then rearrange the tiles to form a new common word. Do the same with each new word until you arrive at the bottom word. For example, a path from BARK to PLUM is BARK, MARK, RAMP, RUMP, PLUM.

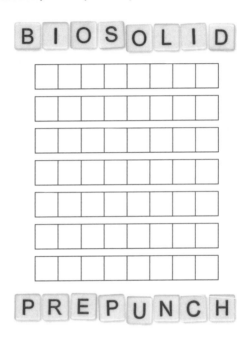

B I O S O L I D

P R E P U N C H

Each of the four-letter words below may be extended both on the right and the left to form a ten-letter word. Drawing from the tiles directly above each word, fill in the blanks to find the longer words as quickly as you can.

A B D E I L R

☐ ☐ ☐ I N C H ☐ ☐ ☐

C E H L O T Y

☐ ☐ ☐ C O L A ☐ ☐ ☐

C C I N O R T

☐ ☐ ☐ T R A D ☐ ☐ ☐

A D E E G M U

☐ ☐ ☐ R A N T ☐ ☐ ☐

A D I M N P S

☐ ☐ ☐ T E R M ☐ ☐ ☐

LEVEL

For each bunch below, rearrange the letters to form two intersecting words that fit into the corresponding grid.

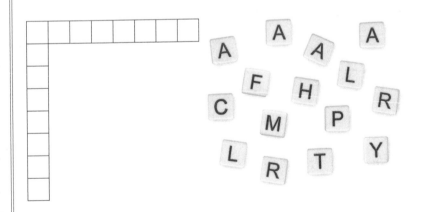

254

For each of the six words below, add one letter from the word LINTER (each letter will be used only once) and then rearrange the letters to spell a word that has three of the same letters. Once you've filled in all the blanks, take the shaded letters from each line and rearrange them to spell a bonus word with three of the same letters.

LINTER

INNOCENT

TETOTUMS

ERECTING

BONUS WORD

MISLABEL

DEBRIDED

ANTIRIOT

BANANA SPLITS

LEVEL

For each of the three words below, change one letter to an E **and then rearrange the letters to spell a type of drink.**

H A B I T A N S

_ _ _ _ _ _ _ _

H O M E L A N D

_ _ _ _ _ _ _ _

S T R O M A T A

_ _ _ _ _ _ _ _

For each of the three words below, change one letter to an A **and then rearrange the letters to spell a word used to describe a person.**

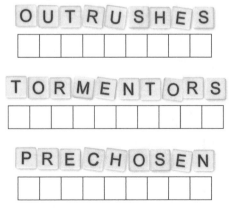

O U T R U S H E S

_ _ _ _ _ _ _ _ _

T O R M E N T O R S

_ _ _ _ _ _ _ _ _ _

P R E C H O S E N

_ _ _ _ _ _ _ _ _

Replace each of the question marks below with one of the five letters V, W, Y, F or H and then rearrange the letters to form a common word. Each of the five letters will be used only once.

A A E G N R U ?

A E E I L T T ?

A A C I R R T ?

A A C D I T U ?

A D I I L N T ?

BANANA TREES

LEVEL

Use the 22 tiles in this bunch to fill in the two grids below. To get you started, a few tiles from the bunch have been placed in each grid. Using the remaining tiles in the bunch, find words that complete each grid.

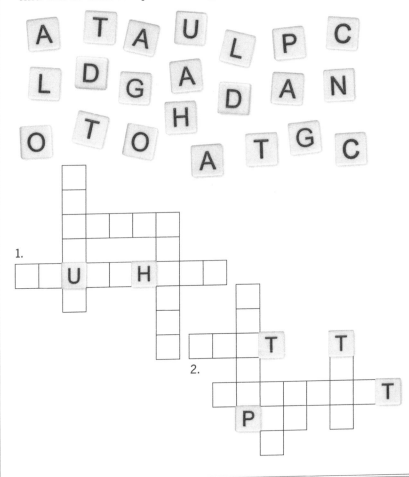

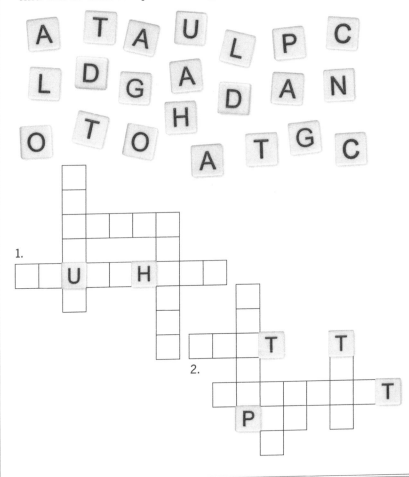

Use the 22 tiles in this bunch to fill in the two grids below. To get you started, a few tiles from the bunch have been placed in each grid. Using the remaining tiles in the bunch, find words that complete each grid.

There is one letter that when added to all of the seven-letter words below can be used to form new eight-letter words. Find the letter that works for all four words, add it to each word, and then rearrange each set of letters to form a new word. For example, L can be added to ROADS, WEARY, EPICS and GONER to form DORSAL, LAWYER, SPLICE and LONGER.

COMMON
LETTER

☐

L A N I A R D

☐☐☐☐☐☐☐☐

B L E A T E R

☐☐☐☐☐☐☐☐

R E A L I T Y

☐☐☐☐☐☐☐☐

I O D I N E S

☐☐☐☐☐☐☐☐

For each of the words below, replace one letter with the tile after the plus sign. Then rearrange the letters to spell a word related to medicine.

N O N E L A S T I C + G

☐☐☐☐☐☐☐☐☐☐

P L A Y A C T I N G S + O

☐☐☐☐☐☐☐☐☐☐☐

C H A T T I N E S S + E

☐☐☐☐☐☐☐☐☐☐☐

I M M O V A B L E S + T

☐☐☐☐☐☐☐☐☐☐☐

I M P R E C I S E + D

☐☐☐☐☐☐☐☐☐

C O R N E T I S T S + B

☐☐☐☐☐☐☐☐☐☐

A D M I S S I O N + G

☐☐☐☐☐☐☐☐☐

BANANA FILLING

Add a P to each of the words below and then rearrange the letters in each word to form a new nine-letter word.

D E B E A R D S

☐ ☐ ☐ ☐ ☐ ☐ ☐ ☐ ☐

C A N O E I N G

☐ ☐ ☐ ☐ ☐ ☐ ☐ ☐ ☐

D E M E A N O R

☐ ☐ ☐ ☐ ☐ ☐ ☐ ☐ ☐

Using any letters EXCEPT the ones that appear in the bunch below, fill in the blanks to form three new words.

N P R

☐ ☐ I N C I D E N T

☐ ☐ A C T I V A T E

☐ ☐ S E N T R I E S

262

Using six of the tiles from each bunch on the left, fill in the blanks on the right to make a nine-letter word that connects the grid.

BUNCH OF BANANAS

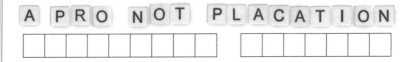

LEVEL

For each word or phrase below, rearrange the letters to spell two names of famous people who both work(ed) in the same field. For example, **HOW TO LIVE STRONG SANE** becomes **ROOSEVELT** and **WASHINGTON**.

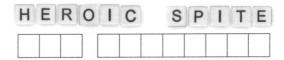

HEROIC   SPITE

☐☐☐☐   ☐☐☐☐☐☐☐☐

A PRO NOT PLACATION

☐☐☐☐☐☐☐☐☐☐   ☐☐☐☐☐☐☐☐

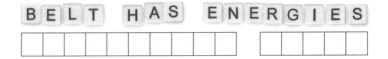

BAR A STAR NO PEACE

☐☐☐☐☐☐☐☐☐☐   ☐☐☐☐☐☐☐

BELT HAS ENERGIES

☐☐☐☐☐☐☐☐☐☐   ☐☐☐☐☐☐

Each set of letters below is arranged alphabetically, and the ? is in the correct alphabetical position. Figure out what letter the ? represents and then rearrange the letters to spell an eight-letter word. For example, in DL?PRUY the ? could be an L, M, N, O or P. Here it represents an O, which can be combined with the other letters to spell PROUDLY.

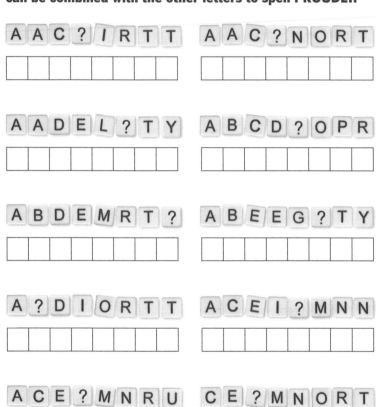

A A C ? I R T T

A A C ? N O R T

A A D E L ? T Y

A B C D ? O P R

A B D E M R T ?

A B E E G ? T Y

A ? D I O R T T

A C E I ? M N N

A C E ? M N R U

C E ? M N O R T

GO BANANAS!

LEVEL

Use all 21 tiles in this bunch to create a collection of connecting and intersecting common words in the grid below. **Each word must contain at least six letters.** The words may be horizontal or vertical, reading left to right or top to bottom.

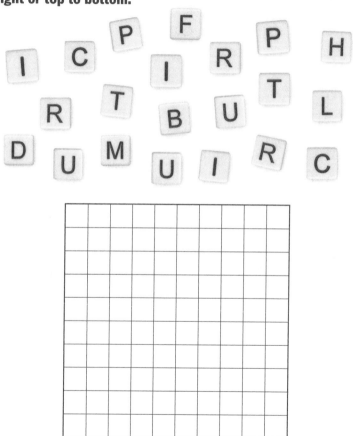

Use all 21 tiles in this bunch to create a collection of connecting and intersecting common words in the grid below. **Each word must contain at least six letters.** The words may be horizontal or vertical, reading left to right or top to bottom.

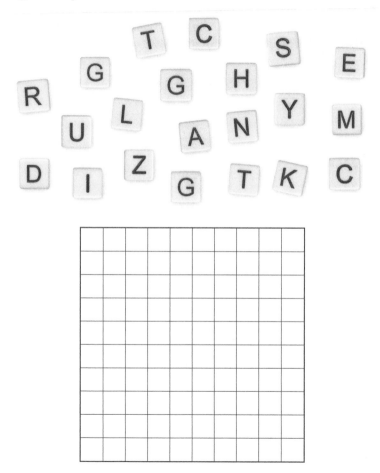

For both of the word groups below, change one letter in the top word to one of the letters that appears in the bottom word, then rearrange the tiles to form a new common word. Do the same with each new word until you arrive at the bottom word. For example, the path from BARK to PLUM is BARK, MARK, RAMP, RUMP, PLUM.

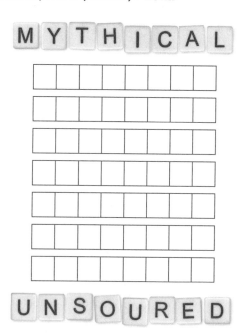

M Y T H I C A L

U N S O U R E D

Each of the four-letter words below may be extended both on the right and the left to form a ten-letter word. Drawing from the tiles directly above each word, fill in the blanks to find the longer words as quickly as you can.

A D I L R S Y

☐ ☐ ☐ P E N S ☐ ☐ ☐

E E I N P R T

☐ ☐ ☐ T A M E ☐ ☐ ☐

A E E L P R T

☐ ☐ ☐ S H O O ☐ ☐ ☐

E I M N S S S

☐ ☐ ☐ G L E N ☐ ☐ ☐

A I L R R S T

☐ ☐ ☐ L A T E ☐ ☐ ☐

ANSWER KEY

PAGE 14

```
  C
  A
  N
  D
S H Y L Y
```

```
        T
        Y
        P
C Y C L E D
```

```
E P O C H
X
A
C
T
```

PAGE 15
HYENA, CAMEL, COUGAR, BEAVER, PORPOISE, HAMSTER

Bonus: ERMINE

PAGE 16
SAMBA, TANGO, SALSA

COLON, CHIN, NECK

PAGE 17
FLAKY, WRECK, HAVEN, AVOID, BEFIT

PAGE 18
1.
```
C R I B
  L I O N
  I
T O P P E D
```

2.
```
      C     B
L O O P   B I T
  P R I N T
  I
  E
  D
```

3.
```
        B
      C O I L
N I     O
I     B O O T E D
P I P E R
        D
```

4.
```
L I N E   D
          E
          P
          I
O R B I T  C
          O
          P
```

PAGE 19
1.
```
B E G
C
H         F
O V A T I O N
          N
          D
```

2.
```
B A C O N
V
O
F I G H T
D     E
      N
```

3.
```
    D
G I V E N
  T
  C
  H O B O
        F A N
```

4.
```
        D
C     G I N
H A B O V E
A     O F
N
T
```

PAGE 20
Common: M; MOTTO, MOUTH, THYME, MOTOR

PAGE 21
PLUM, FIG, CHERRY, ORANGE, LIME, KIWI, PEACH

PAGE 22
BABIED, BEACON, HERBAL, BRACED

PALATE, ADVICE, FUTILE

PAGE 23
BALLAD, LAUNCH

PAGE 24
EEL, BOAR; HEN, CROW; HORSE, ROBIN; FOX, BEAR; DEER, GOAT

PAGE 25
DONUT, FEIGN, LIMBO

FACET, VODKA, PEACE

RATIO, MAXIM, POLKA

TOPAZ, ARMOR, RAYON

PAGE 26
Possible solution:

```
F
I     T W E L V E
F     H
T H I R T E E N
Y     E
      E
```

PAGE 27
Possible solution:

```
          M
          E
V   E A R T H
E         C
N E P T U N E
U         R
S         Y
```

PAGE 28
Possible solutions:
GELD, LEAD, READ, AREA, AURA

PINT, THIN, THAN, BATH, BASH

WARP, PAIR, PITA, PITY, TIDY

PAGE 29
NEATLY, EDITOR, BUREAU, CUTOUT, VIABLE

PAGE 30

```
M A M B O
A
I
Z
E
```

```
F I F T H
A
I
R
Y
```

270

PAGE 31
SPANIEL, TERRIER, GREYHOUND, RETRIEVER, BEAGLE, PINSCHER

Bonus: SETTER

PAGE 32
TUNA, CARP, BASS

SALT, DILL, CLOVE

PAGE 33
HAVOC, AWARE, CANDY, FRANK, RHYME

PAGE 34

1.

2.

3.

4.

PAGE 35

1.

2.

3.

4.

PAGE 36
Common: P; PLUME, INEPT, ADOPT, PANSY

PAGE 37
UTAH, NEVADA, OHIO, KANSAS, OREGON, TEXAS, IDAHO

PAGE 38
RANCID, DEADLY, MALTED, PARDON

SALINE, ARCANE, ASTRAY

PAGE 39
INCOME, UNTOLD

PAGE 40
DOE, ANT; BEE, RAT; CAT, EMU; SNAIL, HOG; ELK, COD

PAGE 41
HUMAN, AWOKE, TRAIT

HARSH, FLAME, MAVEN

CUTIE, ICILY, BLURT

HORDE, OFTEN, MIMIC

PAGE 42
Possible solution:

					D			
					O			
N	I	C	K	E	L			
					L		P	
			Q	U	A	R	T	E	R
					R		N	
							N	
							Y	

PAGE 43
Possible solution:

			C			
			O			
	B	L	U	E	S	
	E		N		O	
	B		T		U	P
	O		R		L	O
	P		Y			P

PAGE 44
Possible solutions:
HOLY, YOLK, KILO, LINK, MINK

HUNG, HANG, GNAW, WARN, WARD

JINX, JOIN, COIN, CORN, CROC

PAGE 45
BRONCO, UNDONE, BYGONE, SUPERB, HOMAGE (or OHMAGE)

PAGE 46

DOUGH / LITZ (DOUGH, and vertically GLITZ)

PAGE 47
GROUSE, OSPREY, CRANE, SANDPIPER, WREN, SNIPE

Bonus: CONDOR

PAGE 48
ACNE, PALSY, RASH

HOUSE, FORT, TOWER

PAGE 49
CHUTE, FLUID, TARDY, WORLD, CLOVE

PAGE 50

1. 

2. 

3. 

4. 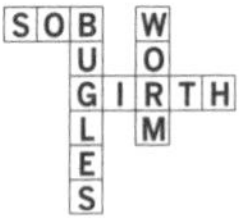

PAGE 51

1. 

2. 

3. 

4. 

PAGE 52
Common: C; CACHE, WENCH, SPACY, CROWD

PAGE 53
PANTS, DRESS, TIE, GLOVES, SOCKS, SHIRT, VEST

PAGE 54
ARCANE, CYMBAL, CATNIP, MASCOT

PEACHY, INROAD, ASSAIL

PAGE 55
ADROIT, MALIGN

PAGE 56
MULE, TOAD; HARE (or RHEA), COLT; STAG, MARE; RAM, VOLE; HOG, TUNA

PAGE 57
BELCH, SIXTH, APRON

ENTRY, WHOLE, LIBEL

GAUGE, AFOUL, COCOA

AGING, VITAL, STASH

PAGE 58
Possible solution:

PAGE 59
Possible solution:

PAGE 60
Possible solutions: BABY, ABLY, FLAY, FLAW, FOWL

GAGA, GALA, GALL, GULL, LULU

WHEW, PHEW, HEMP, HUMP, PUMA

PAGE 61
RUNOFF, FEWEST, SOLACE, FILIAL, TAHINI

PAGE 62

PAGE 63
STURGEON, LAMPREY, STINGRAY, SMELT, SARDINE, FLOUNDER

Bonus: SALMON

PAGE 64
BONSAI, AIKIDO, GEISHA

ADIOS, MACHO, RUMBA

PAGE 65
AFFECT, BEHELD, FLAVOR, FURROW, CLOUDY

PAGE 66

1. 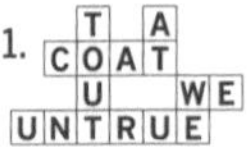

2. 

3. 

4.
```
T U N A
      C
W     U
A U T O
T     E
E
R
```

PAGE 67

1.
```
C     B
A     A   F
A M I D   I
  E     G I G
        E
```

2.
```
    B
    A
M I D I
    A
E G G
    I
  C A F E
```

3.
```
          I
F A   M   C
I     A   E
B A G G E D
          I
```

4.
```
      A
F   M I G
A C I D
    A
    G I B E
    E
```

PAGE 68
Common: L;
REVOLT, HELMET, SULTAN, TAMELY

PAGE 69
STRIKE, PITCHER, HOMER, AVERAGE, STEAL, UMPIRE, STANDS

PAGE 70
COLLAGE, DEGRADE, AGELESS, LONGEST

FRAGILE, REAPING, EXAMINE

PAGE 71
HABITAT, ARRIVAL

PAGE 72
TACO, FRIES;
CORN, OAT;
BEAN, SOUP;
MEAT, RIBS;
TART, BRIE

PAGE 73
COPAY, ANNUL, WACKO

CACTI, DOUBT, SUSHI

UNFIT, RURAL, KAZOO

BURRO, BEIGE, EMBED

PAGE 74
Possible solution:

```
    D     A     F
    R  F R E E R
    Y     M     I
    E R R O R   A
    R     R     R
```

PAGE 75
Possible solution:

```
        A   A
      A R O M A
      E   E
    A N   B
A L O H A   A
    R
    T
    A
```

PAGE 76
Possible solutions:
ADORE, TREAD, TREND, INERT, UNITE, UNFIT

GLITZ, LEGIT, TIGER, GREET, VERGE, VERVE

PATCH, PITCH, TOPIC, PIVOT, DIVOT, VIDEO

PAGE 77
MEANDER, ECLIPSE, AGENDUM, PYRAMID, SOONEST

PAGE 78

```
        H
        O
        N
Z O D I A C
        H
        O
```

```
      I
      M
      P
      R
B O B C A T
      V
```

```
M
A P A T H Y
D
C
A
P
```

PAGE 79
FINGER, STERNUM, SHOULDER, EARLOBE, BLADDER, INTESTINE

Bonus: TENDON

PAGE 80
PASSE, PETITE, ROUGE

TIRED, EAGER, UPSET

PAGE 81
BAGFUL, HEAVEN, BEAUTY, WEAPON, VISUAL

PAGE 82

1.
```
V
E
R
T I     B
  F U R O R
M Y     I
        G
```

2.
```
      R
      O
    R O
F U R T I V E
  G     I
  B     M
  Y
```

3.
```
              F O B
R I M         R
    V I R T U E
    Y       G
```

4.
```
      R
      G U M B O
      I
      T
F I E R Y
      R
```

PAGE 83

1.
```
              G
        M     U
R E R O U T E S
        R     T
        A
        L
```

273

2. REGULAR / TUTU / MORES

3. GLUE / RUMOR / STATURE

4. SUTURE / MATTER / OGLER

PAGE 84
Common: F;
FLAGON, DEFUSE, SAFARI, ARTFUL

PAGE 85
TIGER, LEOPARD, GORILLA, COBRA, ELEPHANT, MONKEY, RHINO

PAGE 86
PATELLA, CENTRAL, BALLAST, DURABLE

DECREED, PLAUDIT, SHALLOW

PAGE 87
OVERACT, LYRICAL

PAGE 88
VEAL, STEW;
RICE, MILK;
CATSUP, ALE;
SODA, ORANGE;
PEA, TOAST

PAGE 89
HOOEY, IMPEL, FETUS

MOGUL, PYGMY, RHYME

BEBOP, EMCEE, MATZO

CHOMP, CYCLE, FLUID

PAGE 90
Possible solution:

LEVEL / LOCAL / LEGAL

PAGE 91
Possible solution:

HONOR / MOTTO / TORSO

PAGE 92
Possible solutions:
FLUKE, KUGEL, GLUED, LODGE, DOGEY, DOGGY

MODEM, MODEL, MODAL, MORAL, ALARM, AURAL

TWEAK, LATKE, DEALT, TILED, FILED, FLUID

PAGE 93
STARTUP, ADDENDA, KILOTON, LEPROSY, BOREDOM

PAGE 94

TIDBIT / CLINIC

NOBODY / COHORT

RHYTHM / TWACK

PAGE 96
POKER, RISK, RACING, GOLF, HEARTS, ARCHERY

Bonus: HOCKEY

PAGE 96
HERNIA, RABIES, PLAGUE

UDDER, SNOUT, POUCH

PAGE 97
FABRIC, VANDAL, ALWAYS, BLEACH, PAWNED

PAGE 98

1. ILK / OBOY / PRIZE

PAGE 99 (right column, top)

2. WOOZY / BILK / PIER

3. POKER / WB / OILY

4. ZOO / YOLK / BERIP

PAGE 99

1. COW / VAPOR / FOUNT

2. CAVORT / FAUN / POW

3. FROWN / GOAT / COPUP / VA

4. VACANT / POOF / OUTGROW

PAGE 100

Common: N;
ONRUSH, SAVANT, NOVICE, INFANT

274

PAGE 101
PHONE, BLENDER, STOVE, FRIDGE, DRYER, RADIO, COMPUTER

PAGE 102
ADMIRAL, STADIUM, CHEMIST, CONSUME

BLASTER, REACTOR, SEASIDE

PAGE 103
ERASURE, SOCIETY

PAGE 104
FISH, LEMON (or MELON); EGG, SUNDAE; BREAD, CARROT; CANDY, APPLE; BAGEL, STEAK

PAGE 105
FUNGI, FOLIO, WRYER

GUAVA, ALOHA, HAIKU

NINTH, LYMPH, RIVET

BORON, VIDEO, CELLO

PAGE 106
Possible solution:

PAGE 107
Possible solution:

			T				
			O	C	T	E	T
			T				
T	I	T	L	E			
	O		M				
	T						
	B	A	T	T	Y		
	L						

PAGE 108
Possible solutions:
MAGIC, AMIGO, DOGMA, MODAL, MOULD, WOULD

CLIPT, TOPIC, TONIC, INTRO, ROBIN, BROWN

COOPT, POOCH, EPOCH, HOPER, HOMER, RHYME

PAGE 109
LOCATOR, NOMADIC, UNHITCH, BELIEVE, CITADEL

PAGE 110

PAGE 111
BELGRADE, SANTIAGO, BALTIMORE, BUCHAREST, BUDAPEST, SINGAPORE

Bonus: BOSTON

PAGE 112
SALAMI, MACARONI, CASINO

PLEASED, TEARFUL, ALARMED

PAGE 113
AFRAID, LAWMAN, VOYAGE, BANISH, SASHAY

PAGE 114
1.

2.

3. HARDEN / DART / SOFTEN

PAGE 115
1.

2. R / AERATES / D / IMPULSE / A / N

3. SUNDAE / L / STAR / A / EMPIRE

PAGE 116
Common: P; PARTAKE, PARTIAL, PROBATE, PROWESS

PAGE 117
ENGINEER, BIOLOGIST, PROSECUTOR, DIRECTOR, SALESMAN, SURGEON, AUTHOR

PAGE 118
BARGAIN, ABSINTH, KNEEPAD, TRANSIT

GYRATING, ARRANGED, OPENABLE

PAGE 119
ANACONDA, ABSTRACT

PAGE 120
RAGWEED, IVY; TULIP, SUMAC; BEGONIA, ASH; LILY, SYCAMORE; BONSAI, ROSE

PAGE 121
TRAUMA,
COWBOY, UNLAID,
AVENUE, AWHILE,
PIGSTY, IMPROV,
TROPHY, GROTTO,
FAMOUS

PAGE 122
Possible solution:

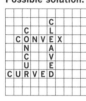

PAGE 123
Possible solution:

PAGE 124
Possible solutions:
ADJURE, UNREAD,
TUNDRA,
OUTRAN,
TOUCAN, COUNTY,
TYCOON

MIMOSA, MIMEOS,
MEMOIR, HOMIER,
HOLIER, HOLDER,
HURDLE

PAGE 125
MEAGERLY,
AISLEWAY,
VIBRANCE,
TABLETOP,
EMPHATIC

PAGE 126

PAGE 127
SKATES,
SUBMARINE,
ESCALATOR,
TRACTOR,
CHARIOT, PLANE
Bonus: TANKER

PAGE 128
COLONEL,
ADMIRAL,
ARSENAL

FORELEG,
ANTLER, STINGER

PAGE 129
CURFEW, HUBRIS,
WALRUS,
ARROYO, TRIVIA

PAGE 130
1.

2.

3.

PAGE 131

1.

2.

3. COPPER
   L
   RAIN
   N
   COTTON

PAGE 132
Common: B;
BRACKET,
BETROTH,
DURABLE,
BEDSIDE

PAGE 133
PRAGUE,
VIENNA, ALBANY,
ISTANBUL, MIAMI,
CAIRO, NAIROBI

PAGE 134
PREPAID,
PAROLEE,
FORCEPS,
ESCAPED

UPDATING,
WRANGLED,
DURATION

PAGE 135
BOUNDARY,
HUMANOID

PAGE 136
ACTOR, FARMER;
TEACHER, MAID;
MAYOR, BUTLER;
DOCTOR, AGENT;
DRIVER, PILOT

PAGE 137
FABRIC, TEACUP,
HOOKUP,
MAYHEM,
STYLUS, OUTWIT,
KIMONO, GATHER,
OUTGUN, MAKEUP

PAGE 138
Possible solution:

PAGE 139
Possible solution:

PAGE 140
Possible solutions:
ZIGZAG, GAZING, CAGING, LACING, CLUING, UNCLOG, COLUMN

CHEEKY, HOCKEY, HOCKED, CORKED, RECORD, DOURER, ARDOUR

PAGE 141
HOLINESS, ARCHAISM, MISLABEL, METALLIC, SYCAMORE

PAGE 142

PAGE 143
CLARINET, TRIANGLE, WHISTLE, HARMONICA, DRUM, HORN
Bonus: CORNET

PAGE 144
SHRINE, CASTLE, PALACE

CHAPATI, SULTAN, EMIRATE

PAGE 145
LEGACY, ANYHOW, FATHOM, SEWAGE, FLAVOR

PAGE 146

1.

2.

3.

PAGE 147

1.

2.

3.

PAGE 148
Common: T:
STALLED, MOBSTER, RECEIPT, STOMACH

PAGE 149
SOLUTION, MOLECULE, NITROGEN, BEAKER, ORGANIC, CARBON, NEUTRON

PAGE 150
CARDIAC, GRANOLA, LYRICAL, MERMAID

PAGE 151
FILAMENT, CHEATING, INFORMED

MEDICINE, FUNCTION

PAGE 152
FELICITY, GINGER; BONNIE, ANGELICA; HEATHER, CAITLIN; CHARLOTTE, AMBER; LAUREL, FLORENCE

PAGE 153
ADVENT; GADFLY; GOALIE; UPTOWN; UNRULY; TURNIP; TWILIT; WHILST; VULGAR; EASILY

PAGE 154
Possible solution:

			W			W			
		W	A	R	T	H	O	G	
			T			I			
			C			L			
		W	H	E	R	E			
			E			D			
			D						

PAGE 155
Possible solution:

								B	
					B			R	
					R			O	
				B	E	A	U	T	Y
					E			H	
			B	E	C	O	M	E	
					H			R	

PAGE 156
Possible solutions:
CONVEY, NOVICE, COINED, IRONED, DINERS, HIDERS, RADISH

FERVOR, FORGER, FORGET, GOITER, TRIAGE, RATING, DATING

PAGE 157
AMBROSIA, ANARCHIC, ABSENTEE, PENUMBRA, ASBESTOS

PAGE 158

PAGE 159
SCOTLAND,
MEXICO,
ENGLAND,
NIGERIA,
AUSTRALIA,
BELARUS

Bonus: RUSSIA

PAGE 160
HOSPITAL,
STADIUM,
REFINERY

ECSTATIC,
HOMESICK,
INSECURE

PAGE 161
SEAWEED,
TYPICAL,
CAVEMAN,
FADEOUT,
IMPEACH

PAGE 162
1.

2. PLAYOFF / CHARIOT

3. PACIFY

PAGE 163
1. PETUNIA / UPFRONT

2. FATIGUE / UNTRUTH

3.

PAGE 164
Common: F;
FLATBED,
CONFIRM,
BEFALLS,
FOREARM

PAGE 165
MICHELLE; Lucy
in the Sky with
DIAMONDS;
NORWEGIAN
Wood;
PAPERBACK
Writer;
SOMETHING;
Yellow
SUBMARINE;
YESTERDAY

PAGE 166
HARDCORE,
COLLAGEN,
TIMECARD

TREATABLE,
ENCLOSURE,
MAINLANDS

PAGE 167
HEMOSTAT,
EDGEWISE

PAGE 168
ANGORA,
OILCLOTH;
BURLAP,
CORDUROY;
FLANNEL,
GINGHAM;
CHAMOIS,
LEATHER

PAGE 169
BALANCE,
NARRATE,
NIRVANA,
UMBRAGE,
DEFICIT,
WEDLOCK,
BLUEJAY,
NEGLECT,
SUFFICE,
UMPTEEN

PAGE 170
Possible solution:

PAGE 171
Possible solution:

PAGE 172
Possible solutions:
AIRPLAY,
PARTIAL,
CAPITAL,
TAPIOCA,
CAPTION,
AUCTION,
CONDUIT,
CONDUCT

UNBLOCK,
GUNLOCK,
UNCLOGS,
LOUNGES,
IGNEOUS,
AGONIES,
SEAMING,
MAGPIES

PAGE 173
ACROBATIC,
BAPTISMAL,
PORCELAIN,
MERCURIAL,
LUCRATIVE

PAGE 174

PAGE 175
FUCHSIA,
CERULEAN,
MUSTARD,
TANGERINE,
MAGENTA,
EMERALD

Bonus: CHESTNUT

PAGE 176
ROSACEA,
TETANUS,
RUBELLA

TORNADOES,
EDUCATOR,
DIORAMA

PAGE 177
CALYPSO,
CROWBAR,
VICEROY,
HEARSAY,
MIDWIFE

PAGE 178
1.

2.

3.

PAGE 179
1.

2. MIDWEEK / TOOTSIE

3. EVOKED / MOTTOS

PAGE 180
Common: Y;
DAYCARE,
CARRYON,
MIDYEAR,
SCYTHES

PAGE 181
Roberto
CLEMENTE; Don
DRYSDALE; Leo
DUROCHER;
Juan MARICHAL;
Christy
MATHEWSON;

Stan MUSIAL;
Willie STARGELL

PAGE 182
SAILBOAT,
CEREBRAL,
RIVERBED

BICOASTAL,
DODECAGON,
INVIOLATE

PAGE 183
COAUTHOR,
MANIFOLD

PAGE 184
ROMANCE, DIARY;
BROCHURE,
BLOG;
NEWSPAPER,
STORY;
MAGAZINE,
REPORT

PAGE 185
HANDBAG,
PARFAIT,
ANTIWAR,
ABUSIVE,
VIBRATE,
MAILBOX,
DISHPAN,
REJOICE,
EPITOME,
FORGIVE

PAGE 186
Possible solution:

PAGE 187
Possible solution:

PAGE 188
Possible solutions:
IMPERIL,
PILGRIM,
PRIMING,
PRICING,
CARPING,
ORGANIC,
GARCONS,
COGNACS

SUMMARY,
YAMMERS,
MASTERY,
HAMSTER,
ATHEISM,
CHEMIST,
CHICEST,
TECHNIC

PAGE 189
CABLEGRAM,
CANDIDATE,
MASSACRED,
POLICEMAN,
CONTAGIUM

PAGE 190

PAGE 191
SHIPMATES, RELATIVES, CHILDREN, ORCHESTRA, TOURISTS, STUDENTS

Bonus: VOLUNTEERS

PAGE 192
VERTIGO, STROKE, RICKETS

CERVANTES, VONNEGUT, NABOKOV

PAGE 193
PRIVACY, BONFIRE, ENTWINE, NAUGHTY, ORCHARD

PAGE 194
1.

PAGE 195
1.

2.

3.

PAGE 196
Common: W; SNOWCAP, RAWHIDE, RENEWAL, WIRETAP

PAGE 197
The APARTMENT; From Here to ETERNITY; The GODFATHER; SLUMDOG Millionaire; Terms of ENDEARMENT; ORDINARY People; UNFORGIVEN

PAGE 198
VERTICAL, ARTISTIC, ANCESTRY

INCITABLE, TRENCHANT, GREASIEST

PAGE 199
DEADLOCK, FLAMENCO

PAGE 200
THE GRAPES OF WRATH, A TALE OF TWO CITIES, THE COLOR PURPLE, ROBINSON CRUSOE

PAGE 201
BARGAIN, ASHTRAY, ABSENCE, PLATEAU, CAYENNE, OUTPACE, RIPCORD, LETTUCE, REVELRY, INFERNO

PAGE 202
Possible solution:

PAGE 203
Possible solution:

					B			
					O			
			J	O	N	E	S	
					D		H	
							A	
			F				N	
		R	I	P	L	E	Y	
			N					
			C					
			H					

PAGE 204
Possible solutions:
HUNDRED, THUNDER, UNEARTH, ANOTHER, TREASON, MATRONS, FORMATS, FLOTSAM

ODOROUS, OUTDOOR, OUTRODE, COURTED, OUTRACE, CENTAUR, CENTRAL, LATENCY

PAGE 205
STATEWIDE, CARPETBAG, CARETAKER, SYNCOPATE, DEFEATISM

PAGE 206

```
E
C
O U T B O U N D
N
O
M
I
C
```

PAGE 207
LOVEBIRD,
ANTEATER,
DINOSAUR,
WATERFOWL,
MARSUPIAL,
POLECAT

Bonus: IMPALA

PAGE 208
RENEGADE,
SOMBRERO,
CAFETERIA

FARMHOUSE,
SYNAGOGUE,
CONSULATE

PAGE 209
FASTBALL,
HAIRLINE,
VIGILANT,
WEAKLING,
STRATEGY

PAGE 210

```
1. D O W N P O U R
   D           N
   D           O
   E           P
   S           E
   T I N M A N
```

```
       W
       E
       A
2. N O N P R I N T
       O       O
       N       D
   U M P S     D
               E
               D
```

PAGE 211

```
1. N E C K W E A R
   I           F
   G           G
   H           H
   T           A
   Y E O M A N
```

```
             A
2. M O R T G A G E
       H E
         N
       W H A C K
   F I N E   Y
```

PAGE 212
Common: G;
MADRIGAL,
GADGETRY,
ESCARGOT,
ENLARGED

PAGE 213
TELEVISION,
SKATEBOARD,
PACEMAKER,
GUILLOTINE,
HELICOPTER,
MOUSETRAP,
POLYESTER

PAGE 214
CATHEDRAL,
AMPERSAND,
LANDSCAPE

COOPERATED,
DEBASEMENT,
INSOLVABLE

PAGE 215
ORANGUTAN,
CAMERAMAN

PAGE 216
OBSERVANT,
UNAWARE;
DANGEROUS,
SAFE; DRAMATIC,
MUNDANE;

COMPLICATED,
SIMPLE;
BEAUTIFUL, UGLY

PAGE 217
SECURITY,
SHORTCUT,
SCORNFUL,
BULLFROG,
SOMBRERO,
BLOWPIPE,
HOMEWORK,
PAVILION,
SOUTHPAW,
WHIPLASH

PAGE 218
Possible solution:

					B			
	O				U			
A	U	D	I	T	O	R	I	U M
	I				E			
	O				A			
	U				U			
	S				S			

PAGE 219
Possible solution:

	B	R	O	U	H	A	H A
			O				
			O				
B	A	R	B	A	R	O	U S
			A				
			Y				

PAGE 220
Possible solutions:
ILLUSION,
ALLUSION,
UNSOCIAL,
CAUTIONS,
CANOEIST,
DISTANCE,
SNATCHED,
DETACHES,
DETACHED

PAGE 221
AFICIONADO,
BALLISTICS,
CENTIMETER,
GENEROSITY,
IMPOVERISH

PAGE 222

```
B
I
R
D
B
M A R K D O W N
T
H
```

```
             B
B I R T H D A Y
         N
         K
         R
         U
         P
         T
```

PAGE 223
NETWORK,
DOWNTIME,
SUBMENUS,
KILOBYTE,
TRUNCATE,
SECURITY

Bonus: KEYBOARD

PAGE 224
DEMENTIA,
GANGRENE,
TINNITUS

MAGNOLIA,
NASHVILLE,
GOODFELLAS

PAGE 225
FILTRATE,
CHILDREN,
INVASIVE,
UNWIELDY,
SYLLABUS

PAGE 226

1.

PAGE 227

1.

2.

PAGE 228

Common: D;
HOMELAND,
DEADBOLT,
IRONCLAD,
DICTATOR

PAGE 229

CATERPILLAR,
MEALYBUG,
FIREFLY,
DRAGONFLY,
CENTIPEDE,
SCORPION,
BUTTERFLY

PAGE 230

SCAPEGOAT,
DISPARAGE,
DETERGENT

THREADIEST,
RELAXATION,
PATROLLING

PAGE 231

LAMEBRAIN,
ANTIPASTO

PAGE 232

ROTTEN,
DENMARK
(Shakespeare's
Hamlet:
"Something is rotten in the state of
Denmark"); TOTO,
KANSAS (Dorothy
from *Wizard of
Oz*: "Toto, I have a
feeling we're not in
Kansas anymore");
LIVER, CHIANTI
(Hannibal Lecter
from *Silence of
the Lambs*: "I ate
his liver with some
fava beans and
a nice Chianti");
ELEMENTARY,
WATSON
(Sherlock Holmes:
"Elementary, my
dear Watson")

PAGE 233

DAYDREAM,
GRADUATE,
GANGLAND,
PEGBOARD,
BADMOUTH,
MEMBRANE,
SPITBALL,
POSTCARD,
CLASSIFY,
LUSCIOUS

PAGE 234
Possible solution:

PAGE 235
Possible solution:

PAGE 236
Possible solutions:
PANORAMA,
PARANOIA,
PARANOID,
DIASPORA,
PARODIES,
TRAIPSED,
DISPUTER,
DETRITUS,
DUETTIST

PAGE 237

APOLOGETIC,
BOTHERSOME,
FELLOWSHIP,
FREELANCER,
HEREDITARY

PAGE 238

PAGE 239

CASELOAD,
BAILSMAN,
RETAINER,
LITIGANT,
MISTRIAL,
LARCENY

Bonus: ALIMONY

PAGE 240

GOATHERD,
DEADBEAT,
RACEWALK

SCRAPBOOK,
MOUSETRAP,
OPERAGOER.

PAGE 241

LEFTWARD,
HANDPICK,
MEATLOAF,
NOSEDIVE,
TREASURY

PAGE 242

1.

2.

PAGE 243

1.

ICEBOUND / CHOOT (vertical) / FRYPAN with vertical NKID

2.

BOYFRIEND / OOTUN (vertical) / HANDPICK

PAGE 244
Common: M;
SPACEMAN,
LANDMASS,
MEGASTAR,
GOURMAND

PAGE 245
BELLADONNA,
AMARYLLIS,
NASTURTIUM,
EUCALYPTUS,
GLADIOLUS,
MAGNOLIA,
HYDRANGEA

PAGE 246
SACRAMENT,
NAMEPLATE,
POLEMICAL

OUTRIGGERS,
DEGENERATE,
STRATIFIED

PAGE 247
NEWSBREAK,
POWERBOAT

PAGE 248
SYNONYMS,
COLOSSAL;
OPPONENT,
BARBWIRE;
CHITCHAT,
ANNOTATE;
DISORDER,
ENSCONCE

PAGE 249
ANYPLACE,
HEADLAMP,
AIRSTRIP,
RHUMBAED,
OBSIDIAN,
SEABORNE,
BANKRUPT,
MACKEREL,
SURGICAL,
SHAMROCK

PAGE 250
Possible solution:

			J		W				
		F	I	N	I	C	K	Y	
			N		Z				
		O	X	T	A	I	L		
			E		R				
			D		D				

PAGE 251
Possible solution:

			T					
	T	R	A	F	F	I	C	
			R			O		
			I			F		
			F			F		
		O	F	F	I	C	E	
						E		

PAGE 252
Possible solutions:
BIOSOLID,
BLOODIES,
POOLSIDE,
POLISHED,
SIPHONED,
PUNISHED,
PUNISHER,
PUNCHIER,
PREPUNCH

PAGE 253
BRAINCHILD,
CHOCOLATEY,
CONTRADICT,
GUARANTEED,
MASTERMIND

PAGE 254

BREETREN (vertical) / FLYWHEEL

PHARMACY / RATFALL (vertical)

PAGE 255
CONTINENT,
UTTERMOST,
ENERGETIC,
SLIMEBALL,
BEDRIDDEN,
INITIATOR

Bonus:
CELEBRATE

PAGE 256
ABSINTHE,
LEMONADE,
AMARETTO

AUTHORESS,
ASTRONOMER,
CHAPERONE

PAGE 257
HARANGUE,
LEVITATE,
AIRCRAFT,
AUDACITY,
TAILWIND

PAGE 258

CATG / TOTAL / LAUNCHPAD with DOOG

GA / HALT / COCOANUT / PAD

PAGE 259

1.

LATECOMER / WENTHETA / YY

2.

HIDEAWAY / OOCTE / MELTER / NTY

PAGE 260
Common: C:
CARDINAL,
BRACELET,
LITERACY,
DECISION

PAGE 261
CONGENITAL,
ANGIOPLASTY,
ANESTHETIC,
METABOLISM,
EPIDERMIS,
OBSTETRICS,
DIAGNOSIS

PAGE 262
BEDSPREAD,
POIGNANCE,
PROMENADE

COINCIDENT, DEACTIVATE, MISENTRIES

PAGE 263
HEADPHONE, WAREHOUSE

PAGE 264
POE, CHRISTIE; TARANTINO, COPPOLA; BONAPARTE, CAESAR; HEISENBERG, TESLA

PAGE 265
ARTIFACT, RAINCOAT, PLAYDATE, BACKDROP, DRUMBEAT, MEGABYTE, DICTATOR, NICKNAME, MANICURE, INTERCOM

PAGE 266
Possible solution:

```
        C
  T R I U M P H
        P   U
        F   T
      R U B R I C
        L   I
            D
```

PAGE 267
Possible solution:

```
              C
      L       H
  D R U M S T I C K
      G       N
      G       T
      A       Z
      G       Y
      E
```

PAGE 268
Possible solutions:
MYTHICAL, MYSTICAL, CLIMATES, ARTICLES, CLOISTER, OUTCRIES, ROUTINES, ROUNDEST, UNSOURED

PAGE 269
DISPENSARY, PENTAMETER, PEASHOOTER, SINGLENESS, TRILATERAL

THE AUTHORS

BANANAGRAMS

Bananagrams is a family company. Abe Nathanson, along with his daughter Rena and his grandchildren Aaron and Ava, invented the game while spending the summer of 2005 together in Narragansett, Rhode Island. Even though they'd created Bananagrams just for fun, they soon decided—after some encouragement from friends—to try selling it. It debuted at the 2006 London Toy Fair and quickly became an international sensation. The whole family is actively involved in the growing company. They live both in the U.K. and in Providence, Rhode Island, where Abe runs the office.

JOE EDLEY

Joe Edley lives for word games. He's an expert Bananagrammer and the author of *Bananagrams! The Official Book* and *More Bananagrams!* He is the only three-time National Scrabble Champion (1980, 1992, 2000), and since 1988 he's been the Director of Clubs and Tournaments for the National Scrabble Association. In that role, he has created thousands of word puzzles to entertain the readers of *The Scrabble News.* Joe also writes a syndicated newspaper column, "Scrabblegrams," and teaches at Scrabble events across the country. He lives with his family on Long Island.